I'm not saying that Bob Stannard is the "Gabriel Garcia Marquez of Vermont," but now that I mention it I have to say that "How To Survive the Recovery, a Vermont Perspective" sort of makes me think that way, and like the way that sounds.

In addition to a successful career in Vermont state politics that lasted over 30 years, Stannard happens to be a killer blues harmonica master, an endearing and well-honed curmudgeon, and a great storyteller. From first-person accounts of Hurricane Irene (a historic devastator that slammed Vermont in 2011) to humorous and touching tales of small-town Vermont living in a time that's not-quite-gone-by, Bob invites us all in and serves up a banquet of delicious stories, while managing to show us how to try and rescue ourselves from the so-called Economic Recovery. I laughed, I cried...and then I double-checked my safe deposit box!

- Robert Resnik;
author and host of VPR's "All the Traditions"

How to Survive the

Recovery

A Vermont Perspective

By Bob Stannard

SHIRES⚫PRESS

4869 Main Street
P.O. Box 2200
Manchester Center, VT 05255
www.northshire.com

How to Survive the Recovery
A Vermont Perspective
©2014 Bob Stannard
Illustrations ©2014 Jeff Danziger

ISBN: 978-1-60571-232-1

Building Community, One Book at a Time
A family-owned, independent bookstore in
Manchester Ctr., VT, since 1976 and Saratoga Springs, NY since 2013.
We are committed to excellence in bookselling.
The Northshire Bookstore's mission is to serve as a resource for
information, ideas, and entertainment while honoring the needs
of customers, staff, and community.

Printed in the United States of America

Dedication

This book is dedicated to my grandchildren: Thyra Grayce and
James Zachariah Hairston, and Ernest Kyaw Win and Ada Khin
Khin Oo Stannard and Azariah Esch Hinnant .

In addition I would also like to dedicate this book to their
parents, Meredith & Danny Hairston, Wesley and May Oo
Stannard and Marlan Hinnant and Simora Hall

TABLE OF CONTENTS

Introduction

INTRODUCTION

I know what you're thinking. You're sitting around saying to yourself, "Geez, Bob, when are you ever going to write another book and help us out here on the economic recovery?"

Notwithstanding the fact that my wife, Alison, is pretty well convinced that I'm deafer than an old dog, I can say today with great conviction, "I HEAR YOU." It's a damned good thing that I do too because if you think the recession was tough, wait until you try surviving the recovery.

The United States economic recovery reminds older gents like me of the famous line uttered by an undisclosed major back during the Viet Nam War, in which he allegedly said, "It became necessary to destroy the town to save it."

It's heartwarming to see that so little changes in our life. As one who finally qualifies for being an old person, I can attest to the fact that old people don't much like change. We like things just the way they are; or perhaps it's more appropriately stated that we like them just the way they were. Things were always better yesterday. If only we hadn't invented that bloody telephone. We were getting along just fine without that damned thing. Hell, all you had to do was to don your snowshoes and hike two miles through the fields and forests over to your neighbor's house to tell him whatever it was that was on your mind. Of course, trudging through the snow for a couple of hours does force one into running the risk of forgetting what it was that was so darned important that you felt you had to leave your warm house and go chat with your neighbor to begin with, which explains why no one ever left their house in the wintertime in Vermont.

But let's get back to the economy for a minute. Hopefully, you've all had a chance to read "How to Survive the Recession – A Vermont Perspective." There's nothing worse than watching a sequel without having seen the original movie. That said, if you've not read "How to Survive the Recession – A Vermont Perspective" yet, then I would suggest that you stop reading right now; go to your local bookstore and get a copy of that book and read it first. There is so much valuable information in that book that it would be a shame to lose the benefit of its wisdom. As we like to say here in Vermont, "There ain't no point in running a road race with only one leg."

Those of you who are from Vermont will undoubtedly not recognize this old saying because, as you know, Vermonters don't run. If the barn is on fire then perhaps they might, maybe, pick up the pace to a somewhat smart stroll; but run?? Never.

About the only thing Vermont has in common with the other 49 states is that we somehow ended up in the Union back in 1791. Although the people of this small, rural state played a major role in the formation of the United States during the Revolutionary War, we were somewhat reluctant to surrender our independence and join the other 13 original colonies. Hey, can you blame us? Vermont was given away by both New Hampshire and New York. It was the bastard stepchild of New England until the rest of the world discovered that we make THE best maple syrup on the planet.

Many Vermonters believe that we are still recovering from having agreed to join the 13 colonies. So, there you have it. There should be no greater authority on recovering than Vermont. We've been at it longer than anyone. We've got recovery down cold. Well, OK, maybe we've got cold down slightly better, but still, damn it, we're pretty good at it.

Having said all that, let's take a look at where we are today. For those of you who have lived in a cave for the past decade, it will come as a bit of surprise that back in 2007 the world's economy just about shit the bed. I mean, like no joke here. The administration of that era pretty much turned a blind eye to what bankers were doing. The goal was simply to make money, a lot of money, and do in any way that they saw fit.

[2]

Say what you will about Wall Street Bankers, but those boys sure do know how to make a buck. OK, so maybe they do it at the expense of each and every one of us, but let's give credit where credit is due (and these guys do know a little bit about credit, too).

Only in America could you possibly have a scenario where those who nearly drove the busload of kids off the cliff be rewarded with fifty more cases of beer; not five, but fifty. Yup, as one president was leaving office, he graciously put together a plan with his Treasury Secretary, who was once, believe it or not, the head of Goldman Sachs; arguably one of the main culprits in our near economic demise.

They mercifully left a burning bag filled with dog pooh right on the doorstep of the incoming president and said, "Not to worry! Just follow this plan and you'll be back on top in no time."

By now this new president has probably come to see that "no time" was being referenced in more of a geological time frame. Turned out the plan was about half as big as the problem, which of course allowed the administration that oversaw the problem to declare that they tried to fix it, but the new guy screwed it up. Thus, all was right with the world. Well, someone's world, anyway.

Most likely not your world though, right? You will recall that the book preceding this one was directed towards you folks who had made millions and invested every dime with Bernie Madoff (arguably THE most appropriate last name of all-time). You ended up basically impoverished, which was a good thing, because now that you've lost everything you can finally get on with understanding what life is all about; life as a Vermonter, that is.

You see, Vermonters deal with recovery all the time and have done so for generations. Basically, it's all we do here, which is why we do it so well. We recover from winter every year. We recover from floods (we really had a chance to shine when Tropical Storm Irene ravaged the place), We recover from whatever it is life tosses at us. Typically, we survive the act of recovery with very little fanfare, which is why you, oh tourist-out-of-state-flatlander-reader struggle with trying to relate. Most people would react to recovering from anything with a great show of pride, accomplishment, and possibly Chinese fireworks. In Vermont we just move on like it was just another day.

I can already see that you're having some difficulty coming to grips with just how all this recovery business works. I'm doing the best I can to try to explain it all to you, but you must appreciate just how hard it is to explain the DNA of a group of people to strangers (of which you, presumably, are one).

Vermonters are not about peaks and valleys. They're more like a barely wavy line. To the untrained observer the line might almost appear to be flat, but believe me it's not. There a little wave to it. You may have to look real close; maybe even with a magnifying glass, but it's there. Hold it up to the light a little and turn. There you go. You see it now?

OK, maybe not. It's a struggle. I get that. So, maybe this story of a tragic event, along with its severely understated recovery, might better help you to understand how Vermonters deal with crisis.

CHAPTER 1

The Garbage Man

There's a store in a little Vermont town known as the Dorset Union Store. Nobody from the town calls it by that name. To the locals the store has always been known as Peltier's Market. It was started by a man named Perry Peltier. He was a quiet guy. He used to wear those arm bands that butchers would wear to keep the sleeves of his starched, white shirt from falling onto the bloody meat he would butcher at the back counter.

The store oozes yesterday. The floors lost their luster long ago and that's a good thing. Today, the place is a little more upscale than it once was, but then again what isn't really? By the late 1970's the store had been purchased by my old friend, Jay Hathaway. With the help from some local investors Jay bought it from Perry. Jay ran the place very well; somewhat different from Perry, but he did a nice job.

There were a great cast of characters who were around back then, not the least of which was Dorset's retired garbage man, Dave Baker. Dave did a lot of different things. Actually, he could be seen as a role model for all young Vermont kids. I don't think he had much in the way of a formal education, which was a good thing. A formal education would've really held him back in so many ways.

Nope, instead he was an A+ student in life. It's fair to say that just about everything Dave ever learned of any value he learned from fishing. Now, this may not make much sense to you, but then again you're the one who lost their ass in the Great Recession, so you'd be well served to listen up here. Although it'd be hard to prove I think Dave, unlike you, had the first dollar he ever made right up until the day he died.

Anyway, about fishing, recessions and recoveries. If you don't fish start doing so right now. Well, today it's about zero degrees out so you might wait until the season starts, but you could spend the time between now and then learning how to fish. No, don't go getting one of those fancy fly rods and $10,000 worth of gear. That's part of the reason we went in the hole to begin with. All you need is a cheap rod, some worms, some beer, some time and some patience. I might suggest that you copy that last line, print it out and hang it on your wall so that you can read it every day. Those few things will keep you out of just about any fiscal trouble imaginable; with the possible exception of the beer. Notice I said, "some beer"; not all the beer in the goddamn store.

After knowing Dave my entire life, (he was the garbage man, after all, and it wasn't like we had TWO garbage men in Dorset back in the 50's and 60's) I finally got an invitation to go fishing with him. This man not sound like much to you, but it would be the equivalent of you getting a phone call from the President's office asking you over for some soup. Suffice it to say that it was about the biggest deal of my life.

We got to the Mettowee River late in the day. Frankly I thought it was a little early and said so to Dave. He replied, "If you do this right it shouldn't matter what time of day it is".

Now I had to ponder on that for a while. I was an enthusiastic fisherman, but my record of bringing home strings of fish was, shall we say, dismal.

Dave said, "Go ahead and bait your hook and toss in right there underneath that overhanging branch. Don't get hung up in the branch." Good advice, but nearly impossible to follow. I grabbed the biggest worm I could find and jabbed the hook through one end of the worm (if you're wincing here I'm not sure that you have the stomach to face the Recovery), bunched up my worm and ran the hook through a second time. No way was that worm coming off my hook.

"You catch a lot of fish baitin' your hook like that?" he asked.

"Uh, well, um, er, some, yeah", I replied.

"Huh, well that's pretty good. I never had much luck catching fish baiting my hook that way. You must be pretty good", he said.

I'm trying to crawl into my boots at this point. Fact is I wasn't very good, but pride is tough thing to overcome. Just ask former President George Bush. I asked Dave how he baited his hook.

"Well, first thing is I look for a smaller worm (damn). Then I place the tip of my hook right on the very end of the worm and carefully slide the worm onto the hook. This does two things. First, I think it's a little easier on the worm. Next, it's a much better way to catch fish."

Now, not only am I a lousy, unsuccessful fisherman, but I'm a worm-torturer to boot. Wonderful. I baited my hook just like Dave showed me. He's about 30 feet away from me, downstream. I'm casting away not catching shit. He had two fish in about three minutes. I looked to see if I had a bite and he had another fish.

I figured it like this. Some guys are babe magnets. Doesn't matter what they do women just want them. I think it was the same for trout. After a while I wondered why he even bothered to bait his hook. Hell, I think the fish would just jump out of the water and into his creel. All he had to do was to sit there and drink a beer or two and not be bothered by the fish at all.

As you might have guessed there's a little more to it than just baiting the hook just right. Once in the water the worm needs to be convincing or you're never going to catch a half-dozen trout in the middle of the afternoon. In case you're wondering I did catch one to his six. It was pretty humiliating nonetheless. If he even noticed Dave didn't seem to care all that much. He probably figured that I was being polite and leaving the fish for him the next time he went out.

Dave's long gone now, but about once a year I'll go back to the same place and just sit there for a while. I'll bring some worms, some beer (not that I'm allowed to drink that much these days; hooray for diabetes) and try to trick those fish into thinking I'm Dave. It doesn't work at all, but it is time well spent.

OK, so back to Peltier's Market. Sorry, the fishing stuff really has nothing to do with surviving the recovery, but I thought it might be helpful for you to get a picture of Dave. He was the calmest, least excitable character I think I've ever known. We often would wonder that if we set his pant leg on fire would he do anything other than look down at it; maybe brush it off with his hand. Dave was a real Vermonter; make no mistake about that.

It's a lovely mid-summer morning. One of those days that you can tell right off it's going to be a hot one by 2:00 p.m. It's a good idea to get to work early before the sun burns you to a crisp. I was mowing lawns back then. My days generally began with a quick stop at Peltier's for a coffee before we went off to mow twenty-five plus lawns that day. Today was no different.

I walked into Peltier's and could see Jay in the back cutting meat (minus the armbands. Yes, times change). I poured a coffee and said good morning to Jay. Seven A.M. in Peltier's is a busy time and there were people already getting their paper and a few items for the day. What happened next happened very quickly.

I said goodbye to Jay and turned around to face the door going out (well, there's only one door actually so it could've been the door going in). There was a well-heeled lady with an armload of stuff about twelve feet away. She was about halfway between me and the door. Through the dusty, dirty glass in the door I could see Dave Baker putting his hand on the time-worn door handle. He pushed the door open and placed his left foot inside the store.

At that exact moment Ms. Well-Heeled screamed at the top of her lungs scaring the living shit out of everyone in the store. It wasn't just a regular scream. Nosiree. It was more like that blood-curdling scream that Donald Sutherland let out in the final scene of "Invasion of the Body Snatchers". No one had any idea what it was that set her off. No one except Dave the Garbage Man. In an instant that lasted for an eternity Dave looked up into the face of the shrieking lady. He could instantly tell that her eyes were affixed on the floor. His eyes shot down to the floor where he saw a most frantic mouse darting back and forth. The mouse was presumably equally as startled as everyone else in the store, based on the way he was running around.

Without any thought, planning or contemplation Dave raised his right leg, which donned a monster big work boot that he most likely bought from H.N. Williams Department Store and slammed his foot back down on the floor. Unfortunately for the mouse (and anyone else who happened to witness this massacre) he happened to be dead center under Dave's boot.

Dave then picked up his left foot and placed it in front of his right foot taking his full second step into the store. Ms. Well-Heeled had the same look on her face as the lady who sat next to you the first time you saw the shower scene in the movie "Psycho". You could've parked a small, European car in her gapping mouth.

Eyes straight ahead, his face void of expression, Dave took his next step. The moment some of us had been waiting for. As his right foot came up we could see what we left of the unfortunate mouse. He was about as thick as a Bicycle Playing Card. There was a giant splotch of blood and body parts that seemed of an extraordinary size considering the fact that the mouse wasn't all that big. Could all of that have come from that tiny mouse? Guess so.

Ms. Well-Heeled had all she could do to keep from throwing up. Notwithstanding the fact that we were all in a bit of a state of shock had all we could to keep from bursting out loud with laughter. Now, don't get me wrong. We weren't all that overjoyed with the demise of poor Stuart Little, mind you, but we all did pretty much enjoy the cool, calm and relaxed way in which Dave the Garbage Man quickly assessed and then disposed of what one lady perceived as an emergency situation. Dave never broke his stride. He just kept walking like nothing had ever happened. There had never been a scream from hell. There had never been a mouse. He was just walking in to get a coffee; just like we all did every day at around 7:00 a.m. Just another day for Dave.

CHAPTER 2

Mom's Recovery

We're just getting going and already I can hear what you're saying. "Bob, what the hell does baiting a hook and stomping a poor mouse flat as a pancake have anything in this big old world to do with Surviving the Recession?"

It's dumb questions like this that probably caused you to lose everything you own during the recession and now find yourself trying to figure out just how is it you're going to survive the recovery. Your problem is one of priorities and perspective. First of all, your priorities were all wrong to begin with. You spent most of your life thinking that it was money you needed and that no matter what you did, how hard you worked, you'd never, ever have enough of it. When you did finally start amassing a few bucks, you decided that the next best thing to working was investing; but not just looking for that measly 10% return. No way, that wasn't good enough for you. Nosiree, you had to get at least 20%, maybe 25%. You heard about a guy named Bernie Madoff who was really turning a buck. He was your guy.

Hindsight being what it is, we now know that Bernie did, indeed, know how to turn a buck. He turned it from being your buck to his. He's now doing 150 years in prison and you're broke. Tell me that's not a win-win! That son-of-a-bitch, Madoff, got exactly what he deserved. You, on the other hand, probably didn't really deserve to lose your small fortune, but man, it's a damned good thing you did. Stop and think for a minute of the future that you might have had had it turned out that Bernie wasn't as crooked as they come.

You'd be sitting around every day looking at reports and salivating over how much money you made that day. Before long you'd come to realize that what you made yesterday wasn't nearly enough. You put a call into Bernie and ask him if he couldn't do just a little bit better than 25% return on investment, because damn it, you just can't possibly survive on a paltry 25% ROI. The stress and frustration build more and more each day. Now you need glasses from reading all those reports, which by the way could stand a little larger font, don't you think? You pass by the mirror and can't help but notice those never-before huge, dark circles under both eyes. You're pretty sure they weren't there yesterday. And is my hairline really receding or is that just an illusion.

You've lost your appetite. You haven't had sex in months and could care less. Well, maybe you're starting to care a little, because you're now wondering just how long it'll be before you look like that slimy little creature, Gollum, in the Lord of the Rings movies. That look may not be that far off. Lucky for you at this moment in your life you're not caring much about sex. I could be wrong but I don't Gollum was getting laid all that much. He didn't care either, because he had that golden ring. That golden ring was all that matter; just like all that gold (well, worthless printed paper, but still it seemed the same to you) you had innocently handed over to Bernie Madoff.

Buddy, this was not a good path for you to be on, ya think? I mean, Gollum would not ever win the "Most Outstanding Hair of the Year Award" and you were not all that far away from looking like that dude. So, instead of sitting around pissing and moaning about having lost your tidy little fortune you should start showing a little gratitude. The recession came to your rescue. The recession was your Dudley Do-Right who came and untied you from the railroad tracks when the oncoming train of ill-gotten wealth was sure to be your demise.

Whew, that was close. Now you've been moping around for about five years. You've lost everything. No job. No more money, but the word is that things are picking up. You're in about the best place you could possibly be. Things can only get better and there's no better place to be than on the bottom when things are going up.

According to the experts, the recession only lasted from 2007 to 2009. Fortunately, the only people who thought that this was true were the experts. Everyone else seems to be convinced that

[15]

we still are in a recession, which does have some benefits in that it makes my first book, "How to Survive the Recession – A Vermont Perspective" continue to be relevant and a number one best seller (well maybe in Manchester).

As you contemplate how best to survive the recovery, which granted has been somewhat slow in the making, it might buoy your spirits some to know that there are a lot of folks out there worse off than you. Now, I know what you're thinking here. You're saying to yourself, "Bob, you numbnuts, there is no one worse off than me. I'm in the tank. I'm at the bottom and we're supposed to be recovering here, for Chrissakes."

It's selfish, small-minded thinking like this that got your sorry ass in trouble in the first place. Unfortunately for you (or most of you, anyway) that you never had a chance to meet my mother, Thyra Cecilia Maria Erk, Jr. (yes, there were two). By the time this once active woman was about ready to rock 'n roll on out of here, thanks to the Big-C, she was about 98% crippled up with arthritis. She was wheelchair bound. Lost her ability to drive. Couldn't use her poor fingers because they looked more like twisted thorn apple branches than fingers. Her feet were just a mess making buying shoes a near impossibility. It hurt just to look at her. You just knew that she had to be in constant, never-ending pain.

Yet, every day she would get herself dressed. She had her once flaming red hair now still flaming red hair perfectly quaffed. Women of my mother's era had to get their hair done about once a week. She was dressed to the nines complete with some sort of gaudy brooch that she would wear pinned to her sweater. Complementing her outstanding outfits (and hair) would be her mainstay; her killer smile. She was, arguably, one of the most cheerful people on the planet; god knows why.

She never had a job. She was a classic stay at home mom spending her days trying to keep three sons from ending up in reform school (that's what it was called back in the '50s and

'60s. Yes, I had some friends there). It's not fair to say that she "never" had a job. When she was in her mid-70s, she decided that it might be time to go to work. She worked part-time for the Red Cross driving old people to doctor's appointments.

When we heard that she got this job (naturally, she was very proud of herself and made it a point to make sure that we all knew she actually now had a job) most of us were somewhat baffled. Why, at this stage of the game would you be driving at all, nevertheless driving around other old people?

"Ma, how old are these folks that you're driving around?" I asked.

"Oh, honey, they're at least in their 60s." she replied. You see, to her, sixty was old because (and I don't know this for a fact, but all fingers point to it being true) I don't think she ever got much older than say late 30s, maybe 40. At some point along the trail, she just decided that it was a hell of lot easier being young than it was being old, so being young it is. That's what it's going to be.

Now, she was no fool and she was certainly aware of the fact that her body was crinkling and shriveling up more and more with each passing day. However, if this bothered her at all, it was damn near impossible to notice. She refused to let on that she was ever in pain. She never really seemed to care that she never had more than two nickels to rub together. She was probably a candidate for every social program out there, but only opted to get on board with Medicare when doctor bills started out pacing the light bill.

The few times I would ever mention the fact that her physical situation might not be so hot she would always reply, "Well, yes, I do have some problems, but there are so many other people out there who are having a much harder go at it than I am."

[17]

On a grey day in April, I was asked to attend a meeting with her and her doctor. I didn't much like the sounds of this. Her doctor, Dr. Garcia, was a cancer doctor. She had off handedly mentioned that she hadn't been feeling well, which had to mean that she was practically on fire with all sorts of pain. This caused her to go see one doctor who sent her to another who sent her to Garcia.

Dr. Garcia was a terribly nice man. On this day, he wore a most solemn expression on his face. My not so hot feeling is taking a turn for the worse. Thyra's sitting there in her wheelchair not necessarily jubilant, but not seeming nearly as concerned as Dr. Garcia. The poor doctor finally spoke.

"You have cancer, Mrs. Laird." he said.

"Where?" she asked.

"It's in your lungs, your liver, and your stomach." he said, mostly looking at the floor, but turning his head slightly to the left to give me a most sorrowful glance. I sort of thought that this was what I was going to hear this day, but no matter what you think, there's nothing that can brace you for these words. No, not the words from the chagrined Dr. Garcia; the words from my mom.

"OK, well, this is not good." she said. "But that's OK, because you now, Dr. Garcia, have some work to do." she said sternly while staring right into the poor doctor's eyes.

"I've been a good person. I don't deserve this. You're the doctor, so it's your job to get this out of me. You have to fix it." she demanded.

The Doc looked over at me with eyes that said, "Help me out here."

[18]

I looked at Dr. Garcia and said, "Well Doc, I've known her my whole life. If I were you, I'd get busy trying to figure out just how it is you're going to fix this." He resembled that Indian boy trapped in a boat with the tiger in the movie, "The Life of Pi". I knew the feeling. I was, after all, her son. Inside I was rather enjoying watching the poor doctor twist this way and that looking for a life raft that would take him away from this rather bizarre situation.

"And don't think you're getting off easy," she nearly shouted at me.

Say what? What do I have to do with any of this other than to lend a sympathetic shoulder on which to cry?

"You, my son, Mr. Writer. I want you to write my obituary." she said. She spent about 38 seconds living in the world of denial before spring boarding right into acceptance. It took both me, and the poor doctor, totally by surprise.

"Yeah, OK, Ma. Sure. I can do that." I replied cooperatively hoping that my reflective tone would pretty much shut down this conversation. I was quickly starting to relate to how the poor doctor was feeling. I was not real thrilled to have the white-hot spotlight of my mom shining on me. I had that plenty as a kid growing up. It was occasionally followed closely with an encounter with her hairbrush being placed with great force on my butt. I've never feared going up against anybody, except Thyra. Yes, I am smarter than I look.

"You're not getting it. I want you to write it now." She said, with near fire in her eyes.

"Uh, Ma, when you say "now" you're not talking about, like right here, right now, right? I mean I don't think I even have a pen or anything." I said. (You see, coming right out and saying "No" was not an option. I had to buy some time here.)

With her dazzling eyes darting back to Dr. Get-Me-Outta-Here she said, "How long do I have?"

I think if I had had a pistol with me that day, I would've put Dr. Garcia down. It's what you do with a horse with a broken leg. It's hard, but it is humane.

"Well", he bumbled, "it's really hard to say. Some people can go….."

"I want a number." she said. "How many months?"

Boy, the poor doctor had better hope that she doesn't have a hairbrush stuffed inside that wheelchair or he's dead meat.

"Six months, probably, but it might be less." he said looking as though it was he who was terminal and not the 84 year old woman in front of him.

Snapping her head back in my direction causing me to nearly jump out of my seat she said, "I want my obituary written now, because I want to make sure you say nice things about me."

"Ma, jeez, of course I'll say nice things about you."

"You say that now. Get busy. I'll want to read it right away."

And that ended one of the most awkward doctor visits I'd ever been privy to. As you might imagine, writing someone's obituary while they're still here is, shall we say, a bit odd. By that I mean I just couldn't do it.

Every Sunday we'd call my mom to check in and say "Hi". The conversation always went exactly the same.

"Hi, Mom."

"Hi, Bobby. How are you?"

"I'm fine thanks. You?"

"Oh, I'm fine. How's Alison (my wife)?"

"She's fine."

"How're the kids?"

"They're fine."

"How's Lyla?" (that was our best bad dog in the world; a Boxer. 'Nough said)

"Lyla's fine."

Then here it comes.

"How are you coming on my obituary?"

My stomach would just about fall out on the floor. Thankfully, our skin is a very tough organ or else this would be just an awful mess. I just wanted to hang up the phone, but that, of course, was not an option. Instead, I did what every other son would do when confronted with a mother relentlessly seeking the truth. I lied.

"I'm working on it, Ma"

"YOU'RE LYING. You're my kid. I raised you. I know when you're not telling me the truth. I don't even need to be there to know that you haven't written one word yet, have you?"

Man, this was going to be tough. Six months, eh? How many Sundays is that now?

"Ma, it's really hard to write an obituary while you're still here. It's something you write after the person goes."

[21]

"That's not my problem. You agreed to do this now - get busy." she said. I what? I don't recall agreeing to any such thing. When the hell did I agree to do this? I was totally co-opted. Sure enough, each and every Sunday we'd talk and each and every Sunday the conversation above was repeated damn near word for word.

Now I was raised by two folks who felt that your word was your bond. In this case, I had not actually so much given my word to write this obituary as my mom had believed I had. Belief is a powerful thing, as hopefully you'll come to learn. It didn't matter in the least that I hadn't agreed to do a damn thing. What mattered is that my mom had agreed that I had agreed to do this. I was dead meat.

Believe me when I say that I tried. I started this project God knows how many times. I'd write about one half of one sentence and then stop. My mind would wander back to the good days and I'd get so overwhelmed at what was happening that I couldn't write another letter; say nothing about an entire word.

Sure enough, the day did arrive when she started her decline. It was Saturday, September 3rd, 2005, when she was admitted to the hospital. She could barely speak a complete sentence. By the end of the day she was down to single words. We went to see her on Sunday and she was aware, but all done talking.

I spent the following days with her in the hospital. The staff was great. They set me up with a table for my laptop and provided me with Internet access. It was Monday and I decided that it was about time for me to hold up my end of the agreement, that I had never really agreed to, and begin writing this obituary. Most of that Monday was spent just sitting there staring at the computer screen. I knew the time short, the pressure great, but the brain was still in denial; flat-lined actually.

By Tuesday, I was gaining some, but not enough focus. At one point, I asked one of the nurses if I was just wasting my time being there. Although she was breathing, she appeared to be, for all intents and purposes, gone.

The lovely nurse said, "We do this every day here. Your mom is very much aware of what's happening around her and who is in the room. She's just not able to communicate, but she can hear you and she knows you're here." She stood there for a minute looking at me. I sensed that she wanted to say something more, but something was holding her back. Eye contact allowed her to finish her thoughts.

"We also believe that when a person's body shuts down that their essence remains in the room for a while." she said, looking rather nervous as though maybe she shouldn't have said anything.

"How long?" I asked.

"It's hard to say. It's different with each person but usually around 15 to 20 minutes or so." she sheepishly said.

I found this observation to be most fascinating. In an instant, a moment of great clarity hit me like a lightning bolt. I knew I could do this. I started writing away on a legal pad that I had in my possession for the sole purpose of writing this piece, but never had started. This was one of those times that, as a writer, you get to feel every so often. The words just appear on the paper. They seem to come from a place far, far away. You look at your own fingers and you know that it is you who is doing the writing, but you don't really have a whole lot of say over what's being written. It's coming from somewhere else. If you play music at all, then you've experienced this "high." It's a very cool, albeit somewhat unnerving feeling.

I watched as the obituary unfolded on my pad of paper. When it was done, I went back and re-read it. It read well. I put down my work, reached over and grabbed one of the moist cotton swabs and ran it around Thyra's mouth, a task that I did frequently. The last thing I thought I needed was to run into her in the afterlife and get a real talking to about why I let her mouth get so dang dry while I'm sitting there writing an obituary that I should have written months ago. Yes, I know all about pressure, thanks for asking.

After making sure that she was as comfortable as she could be, I said, "Hey Ma, guess what? I'm holding up my end of the deal. You're still here and I've just finished your obituary." I proceeded to read it to her.

Now, it's wicked hard to tell here, but it did seem as though she might have moved just a hair as I was reading this to her, but then again, it could've been my somewhat over-active imagination. I was feeling very good after reading to her; well, notwithstanding the fact that I was bawling like a baby, of course. But I had held up my end of the deal.

I woke up Wednesday morning feeling an odd sense of urgency. I knew I would be going to the hospital again today, but this was different. This may sound strange, but I was being pulled to get to the hospital. I didn't shower or shave. I threw on the same clothes I had worn the day before (well, I did put on clean underwear. Jeez, if mom had an inkling that I hadn't, I would be such a dead man), hopped in the car and raced the thirty miles north to the hospital.

I walked through the double doors into the wing where people go when they're on their way out. On previous days, the staff would look up and smile and offer a warm welcome. When I walked in the reception area that Wednesday, September 7, 2005, everyone was just a little off. I don't know how else to explain it. They were the same people, just different.

I walked into Mom's room. Something was different here as well.

[24]

"Hey Ma, how we doing today?" I asked. "You're color's a little off, but your hair looks great." (Not complimenting her hair was a huge faux pas that I was not about to make). There are moments in one's life that never seem to end. Time stops or at least slows way, way down. Your reality of one second ago dissolves and you find yourself inside a new reality, one that's not moving very fast at all.

I turned to open the door to get some help. The entire staff was at the door, which startled me back into my old reality. The nurse with whom I had spoken a few days ago was in the front of group.

I looked right at her and asked, "How long has she been gone?"

Tears welled up in her eyes. I could tell it was hard for her to do anything more than just stand there. She mustered up a lot of courage and replied, "She passed about five minutes ago."

Perfect! I knew she was still in the room. I turned around, took my seat that I'd occupied for the past few days, pulled out a "C" Marine Band harmonica and said, "Hey Ma, I don't know if there's any truth to what that young lady said about people hanging around not wanting to leave right off. But if it is true, then let me play this song for you."

The first real song I ever learned to play on a harmonica was a song written by Ann Ronell in 1932; "Willow Weep for Me". It was the fourth song on Charlie Musselwhite's "Memphis" album that he released in 1969, the same year I picked up my first harmonica. It's a most wonderful song. I hope I did it justice on that day.

You're probably thinking the obvious, that my mom never recovered from her illness. If you look at it from a Vermont perspective, you'd realize that she recovered just fine. What

[25]

mattered most was whether or not her hair was perfect. The rest was just white noise.

You're probably wondering just what it was I did end up writing for an obituary for my mom. Here it is along with a picture that ran with it in the papers.

Thyra "Tessie" Stannard Laird

Thyra "Tessie" Stannard Laird moved on peacefully from this world on Wednesday, September 07, 2005. As was the essence of her being, she fought hard against the cancer that taken up residency in her body.

She was born in New York City on April 20, 1924 to Gerhardt Erk and Thyra Cecilia Maria Anderson. She came to Dorset, Vt. with her single mother when she was very young and they lived with John and Lucy Stannard; the parents of her first husband, James P. Stannard, Sr., who preceded her in death 28 years ago.

Those who had the privilege of knowing her came to realize quickly that she was exceptionally strong of character and easily adored. In her early years, she enjoyed skating, horseback riding, singing, and her friends who joined her in her ceramic studio. She was a friend to those in need, generously volunteering her time to the Red Cross driving much younger people to doctor appointments. And, of course, playing her piano. She performed at Carnegie Hall at the age of 14.

[26]

She loved her three sons, James P., Jr., Bob (or Bobby as she insisted on calling him) and Curt with all her heart, which was irreparably broken when Curt passed away on Dec. 13, 2001.

On August 24, 1991, she had the good fortune of marrying the last love of her life, Carleton "Dick" Laird. Two people were never more perfect for each other. They spent many hours camping, fishing and sleeping in their truck.

She is survived by her two sons, Jim and Bob, and numerous grandchildren and great-grandchildren. Perhaps she will best be remembered for her insistence on having her beautiful, red hair done to perfection, her grace and beauty, and her love of teddy bears.

Funeral services will be held at the United Church of Christ in Dorset, Vt. on Friday, September 9th at 2:00 pm. There will be no calling hours. In lieu of flowers, donations/contributions can be made to the Curtis A. Stannard Scholarship Fund c/o Rutland Public Schools, 6 Church St. Rutland, Vt. 05701 Attn: Randy Roberts.

CHAPTER 3

What Goes Up Must Come Down

What is the difference between a Recession and a Recovery from a Recession? That is a very good question. Perhaps an equally good question might be just how does one know when they have come out of a recession and are on their way to letting the good times roll once again?

The entire process is not unlike one great, big, giant fireworks bomb. A fuse is lit igniting the bomb. Whoosh, off it goes straight up into the sky leaving a care-free trail of sparks behind as thousands of people crane their collective necks to look skyward in anticipation of what is about to come. This is the riding high part in which we blast forward, willy-nilly, into a recession because we've been way too busy enjoying the ride up. And what a fast and glorious ride it was.

People were partying like it was 1999! Didn't have nearly enough money to do what you want or get what you want? No problem, that's what credit cards are for. Just load 'em up and don't look back. There's way too much fun on the horizon to be worrying about making that interest payment (lord knows, you're not even contemplating paying down the principle).

Up and up you go with a trail of sparks dancing off your heels. The champagne is flowing and the party's movin' and groovin' along when suddenly KA-BANG. The brightest flash ever surrounds everyone. Red, blue, green, gold, silver. The light is blinding. This must be it. You're doing so great that everything just explodes with joy around you. You're driving a sports car you never could afford and living in a huge house with a mortgage that no one in the mix ever could see how you could possible carry, but the word of the day is "never mind" (OK, so technically that's two words. Keep your comments to yourself. I'm busy making a point here).

You're spending most of your time in the new pool that even your wife was somewhat apprehensive about installing, because she thought it might commit some of the borrowed dollars that she was anticipating using to buy the new mink coat she always wanted. Yessir, things were going just great. Not a care in the world until that big bang went off. What the hell was that noise anyway? That light was so darned bright that you couldn't quite see just what it was that went off, but hey, what the hell; pass the champagne. We're not out of champagne yet, are we?

The bright light of the explosion slowly begins to diminish. It takes a while for your eyes to readjust to the impending darkness; probably just a little too long if the truth be told. The glow of all of those other folks shooting up with you on the way up to the top is starting to fade a little bit, then a little bit more. Hey, wait a minute. There's your buddy right over there. You both bought 8,000 square foot homes in the same week. That can't possibly be his spark fading away into a barely glowing ember. Oh, damn, he's turned into a piece of ash.

You grin a little as you watch him float slowly back down. What a jerk he was. He thought he could one-up you when he bought that Ferrari. That was over the top. How the hell did he ever get a loan for that ride anyway? You knew he was going to burn out.

About the time you're having your devious thoughts about your friend and neighbor, you realize that the bright light surround you is starting to fade, and fade rapidly.

"No, no, this can't be." you cry out to no one in particular, because A) nobody's really listening up there a thousand feet above the ground; and B) everyone around you is too worried about their own demise to give much of a rat's ass about your petty problems.

The colorful lights of your ascent have now gone out. All that's left is the ash slowly making its way back down to the ground. It may even land on some of those poor slogs who were never able to get on that rocket that blasted into the sky. Nope, those folks were left behind. They had to stay with their feet planted firmly on the ground. They were relegated to simply watching you and your friends ride way up there and provide them with a most spectacular, albeit brief show of sparking, colorful light.

The folks on the ground were too broke even for the greedy bankers who couldn't sign people up for the ride fast enough. They were never going to get on board. Oh sure, some of them were able to get their hands on a credit card and sail right through to the maximum limit in no time, but their maximum limit didn't hold a candle to your maximum limit. Nope, for the most part, they just had to wait behind.

Unfortunately for you, their behind is what you will now be looking at and maybe for quite a while. As your sad, little ash drifts back to earth, you take a minute to reflect on the glorious, albeit brief ride up. Man, was that ever fun. You had it all (technically you never had squat. Your greedy banker had it all. He bundled it up along with others who thought they, too had it all and sold the bundle, which was then insured by a third party. It was a perfect plan. Or, as we like to say here in Vermont, "What could possibly go wrong?"). You were on your way. You had the baseball cap AND the T-shirt that both read "Life is Good" on the front. And damn it, it WAS good. The problem was that it wasn't really your life. It was just a spark, just a flash in the pan glimmer that provided you with a blast of colorful fun; fun that only last an instant. Fun that you had hoped would last an eternity.

You drift downward. Man, that ground seems to be coming up pretty fast. This landing could hurt some. Not too worry. The only reason the landing would hurt would be because of the weight you're carrying. Fortunately for you all that weight just went up in smoke. You've got nothing left thus allowing you to land gently onto the ground.

Well see, that wasn't so bad after all. At the precise moment that you have this thought, one of those poor bastards who never did get on the ride-of-a-lifetime and lived in a meager home and drove a very well used Subaru with all-season tires because he didn't have enough cash on hand to buy winter tires and his dad taught him that if he didn't have the money in his hand then he shouldn't be buying something he couldn't afford, placed his right foot down onto the ground. Unfortunately, you just happen to have landed just under his foot.

Welcome to the bottom, Phoenix. Remember, out of the ashes rises greatness. Things may seem real dark right now, but you luckily have now landed on the doorstep of World of Recovery. If you thought those lights were bright going up, just wait until you see how bright they'll become now. You see, the brightest light in the world can be a match when lit in a dark cave a mile back underneath a mountain. Let's hope your match isn't wet, because you have some work to do. You have to figure your way out of the mess that you now find yourself in. No, the greedy banker who acted more like a heroin dealer graciously giving you your first fix for free is nowhere to be found. Oh, and don't worry, because the people who were the brains behind this Ponzi scheme did just fine. They figured out a way to get the poor slogs on the bottom to hand over their hard earned tax dollars to them, because they cried that if they didn't get more money the world would come to an end.

Yes, we realize here that this provides you with very little solace inasmuch as your world did come to an end, but jeez, show a little sympathy. Just because you were a fool and ended up in the crapper shouldn't mean that those people who helped put you there should be inconvenienced. Your problem is that you're upset. You just need a little time to recover. Keep in mind what fun you had and what a blazing ride up you had. See, now don't you feel better? You're now on the road to recovery. OK, so the road is completely covered in thumbtacks and you, Mr. Hot Shot, no longer have shoes, but look on the bright side. You are now just about on par with the average Vermonter and those folks have been around for hundreds of years. They haven't burned out yet.

You need to come to grips with the fact that you are one lucky bastard. Yeah, this may take a while. Here, grab my hand. Don't look up at the colorful blast in the sky. That will only depress you. Oh, and careful of the tacks.

CHAPTER 4

A Shot in the Ass

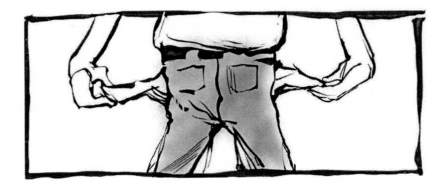

Just reading the title of this chapter should be enough to maybe begin to give you some hope. The blessed Recovery that we are joyfully experiencing is making everyone's life so much better. Things are really picking up and starting to move now. The electricity all around is damned near terrifying. I say terrifying because many of us have had some not altogether positive experiences with electricity. But let's not dwell on the bad times when you put your mom's bobby pin in the outlet or peed on an electric fence (yes, there are some things best left until another time).

Instead, let's focus on the good times. Part of your problem is that you're still in the doldrums at having lost everything you own. This power of negative thinking has gone a very long ways towards diminishing your ability to appreciate the Recovery.

I can hear you blatting away now, "There isn't a goddamn Recovery. After losing my ass, I haven't been able to do anything. I can't find a job because everyone thinks I'm a dumbass for losing a fortune. I'm still living in my car. I haven't got a friend in the world. Jesus-H-Christ, why the hell are we talking about a freakin' Recovery? Are you're nuts?!"

Perhaps, instead of whining about your self-inflicted misfortunes, you might stop for a minute and go back and re-read Chapter 2; the tale about my mother. Remember, no matter how dismal your stinking, rotten, down-in-the-gutter, dismal life is…there's always some poor bastard out there worse off than you.

OK, here you go; "Who the hell can possibly be worse off than me? I was riding high. I was on my way up. I had millions. I had a penthouse in New York City. I had it all. I had the world by the ass!"

Yup, you probably did. But perhaps the only thing worse than having the world by the ass is having your own ass filled with #9 bird shot. If you have never experienced the sensation of having a full load of #9 bird shot hit you square in the ass (and obviously you have not or else you would not be bitching away about simply losing a fortune and referring to that inconsequential act as "losing your ass". There is a difference between metaphorically losing one's ass and losing one's ass) then I might respectfully suggest that you ratchet your whining down a few notches.

It was the summer of 1968. What a great time of life that was. It was such a shame that we didn't appreciate how cool an era it was. Life's a funny thing, isn't it? Here you are coasting right along in the best time ever and you're way too busy using a pair of tweezers to pull bird shot out of your friend's ass to even notice that The Doors are playing "Light My Fire"; and on AM radio, no less.

By 1968, the Viet Nam war was in full swing with the Tet Offensive. President Lyndon Johnson, meanwhile, was calling for the non-conversion of the U.S. dollar. New York City's Madison Square Garden opened. The Civil Rights movement was in full swing. Martin Luther King was shot dead. President Johnson signed the Civil Rights Act (timing is everything). The Beatles started Apple Records (apparently without notifying Steve Jobs). The movie "Rosemary's Baby" was #1 at the drive-in theaters. There were drive-in theaters. Richard Nixon and Spiro Agnew were nominated by the Republican Party as candidates for President and Vice President. The Democrats nominate Hubert Humphrey and Ed Muskie in Chicago. Outside of the convention center, anti-Viet Nam War protestors are going at it with the cops (when was the last time we saw kids this pissed off about a war??). The news show 60 Minutes debuted. Led Zeppelin made their first public appearance, thus changing the world of Rock and Roll forever. Jackie Kennedy married Aristotle Onassis. Nixon beat Humphrey. Pan Am Flight 281 is hijacked and taken to Cuba. Elvis Presley staged a comeback (sort of).

On the radio we were listening to Otis Redding singing "Sitting on the Dock of the Bay" for the first time, and the number one song was "Hey Jude" by the Beatles. Maybe the reason folks in Vermont didn't realize much about what was going on was because there was so much going on. Vermont's a little slower than the rest of the country. Things don't move as fast up here in this little state and when things start swirling around out there throughout the rest of the country (and the world, for that matter) then we tend to slow down even more.

Probably if you drove through Vermont in 1968 what you would have seen would have been a scene similar to that episode in Rod Serling's Twilight Zone; the one where the guy had the stop watch and when he hit the button everyone and everything around him stopped. He had a blast robbing banks and stealing stuff without anyone noticing. Of course, you remember how this guy's story ended, right? He dropped and broke the watch when everything was stopped. He freaked out and lost mind; not unlike the same reaction you exhibited after losing your ass. Had this guy who dropped the watch been a Vermonter, most likely he would have seen his new situation as about the best thing that could've ever happened to him. Hell, if he'd given it two seconds thought, he probably would've smashed the damn watch on purpose just so he wouldn't have to listen to you whine about your demise.

Vermonters get this a lot and it's probably because we're such good listeners. There's nothing worse in the world than being a good listener, because if you're a good listener, then people are inclined to want to talk to you because you'll listen to them; or at least they'll think you're listening. This is why Vermonters are so tough; not just physically, but mentally. The average Vermonter will spend about 9/10's of their life just listening to people bitch about stuff. Here's a typical conversation between someone not from Vermont and a Vermonter.

"You know where I'm from the weather is really quite nice. We don't have a whole lot of snow and it seems like the sun shines a lot more. The weather sucks here."

"Yup".

"Doesn't it ever get any warmer? Where I'm from it's a lot warmer than this. Jesus, it's cold here. Foggy, too. Does it ever clear up and get any warmer?"

"Yup. Nope."

"Where I'm from we have huge factories and housing developments and strip malls. What the hell do you people do here for work?"

{Response preceded by a puzzled expression} "Work?"

"Jesus Christ, are you a freakin' mute?"

"Some say".

And speaking of bitching about stuff, it was the summer of 1968 and my friends and I were practicing shooting skeet. My friends were much older than me; well it seemed that way at the time. I was seventeen. My friends were nine years older than me. That's a lot when you're only seventeen. They can go to bars legally. You have to get a fake ID. The Buchmayr Boys, as they were known throughout southern Vermont and Manhattan, were triplets; two identical and one fraternal. Charlie and Norbert were identical twins easily identified, because Charlie had this big old birthmark right under his left eye. Sig was the fraternal brother and I never thought he looked anything like either of his twin brothers. They were all real handsome, but Sig (or Siggy as he was also known) was scary handsome. His good looks got him in just about as much trouble as it got him out of.

I had come to know these characters because my grandmother, Thyra Cecilia Maria Erk, Sr., was their nanny. My grandmother was ALWAYS referred to as Nanny. I think I was in college when I realized that she had another name and by then it didn't matter all that much.

The Buchmayr Boys were known to hang around with guys like Tony Perry, the man who created the Perry Restaurant Group, but more importantly owned and operated The Five Flies, the hippest bar/restaurant in Manchester at that time. Tony's a big guy with a big voice and oozed confidence. He's one of those guys who's a natural born leader; a man's man. Dashing, smart, funny, and one damned good shot. He was also a whole lot more responsible than the rest of us. This would pay off later.

There was once an airport in Manchester, Vermont. Well, that may be a little extreme. There was a grass strip where pilots with gonads the size of soccer balls would fly in and out of. There was a hanger there which housed a plane or two. Other planes were tied down to the ground. To me that's when they appeared to be the safest. These planes were made of something like canvas and duct tape. The idea of sitting in one while tied safely to the ground was intimidating enough. Leaving the ground was out of the question.

The airport had another function. During the summer months, and in between flights, a group of us would drive up to this wonderfully long, flat spot of earth and shoot skeet. There were no houses around to speak of and it was highly doubtful that the #9 bird shot that we used to practice would travel the distance of the runway. We would drive from the Buchmayr's house, which was no more than a mile away, if that, in their early '60s British Land Rover. This was the quintessential hunting/sporting vehicle of its day. It was painted an interesting color that some referred to as baby-barf-brown. It was somewhere between beige and non-beige. It had the world's most uncomfortable bench seats in the back. However, these bench seats were not like the bench seat the Audi Q5 you had before you lost it. No sir, these bench seats went parallel with the rig. This was important for a variety of reasons. Number one (and perhaps most important) should the driver not be even remotely aware of the road because he was busy scouting for woodchucks, deer, or whatever it was we were looking for on any given day, and unintentionally leave the road and hit an immovable object, the passengers in the back would simultaneously fall on top of each other in a heap of arms and legs all pressed firmly against the back of both the driver's and passenger's front seats. Silly you are probably asking why the seatbelts wouldn't have prohibited this pile up. There were no seatbelts and they would not have been used had there been any. One would not want to be restricted from free movement while riding in this death trap. Generally speaking, one of us always had a hand on the lever that would open the back door in the event that we all had to jump out and begin firing. Knocking heads with your fellow compatriots during an inadvertent car crash was a cheap price to pay for readiness.

The Rover was full of clay pigeons (roughly 1,000) and boxes of bullets (roughly 1,000), shotguns, and men. Every Saturday morning, we would pile in the Rover and head down to Ken's Sport Shop, which was where Manchester Sport Shop still is today (but a much, much different store). Ken would always have our order of 1,000 birds (as clay pigeons are known) ready for us when we arrived. On the box of clay pigeons, written in bright blue letters, were the words, "Don't throw where hogs feed." I could never understand why it didn't say, "Don't SHOOT where hogs feed" but hey, I was kid. What did I know? We didn't buy a lot of ammunition from Ken though. Why buy ammo when you have a 17 year old kid who lives in town and is pretty fast at reloading.

At the end of two days of near non-stop shooting, we would collect all of the spent shotgun shells and put them in the now empty skeet boxes. We would take the spent shells down into the basement of the Buchmayr house where they had a complete reloading shop set up. In the basement were tons of black powder, caps, wadding, #9 bird shot, a crimping machine and a bulb in a socket hanging illegally from the ceiling. (One might argue that although the wiring of the basement was by no means up to code, this might have been the least illegal thing my friends had ever done).

I was able to reload about 250-300 shells per night before I thought my arm was going to fall off. Actually, I imagined that there was a race going on to see whether my arm would fall off before I went blind from the inferior lighting.

Reach in the box. Get an empty shell. Pop out the spent cap in the brass base. Put in a new cap. Dump in the exact amount of black powder (over loading the shells was never a good idea. Charlie told me to always over load the shells.) Pour in the exact amount of #9 bird shot. Put in the wadding and gently pull down on the lever that would crimp everything right into place. Toss that bullet into the box that is so very slowly filling up with live bullets. Then reach over, grab another spent shell and do it all over again.

You see, today kids that are seventeen years old are probably playing the latest version of "Fast & Furious" or just hanging around doing heroin. We never had those luxuries in 1968. Hell, I hadn't even smoked pot yet! Although tedious work, it's fair to say that spending much, if not most of my nights reloading shotgun shells kept me from doing something else that I might regret. By the time Friday rolled around, I would have completed reloading at least 1,000 shells. I usually did an extra hundred or so in the unlikely event I had some misfires. I never had any misfires, which turned out to be tragically unfortunate. Had I had just one bullet that was improperly put together and had that one bullet made its way into the chamber of Siggy's 12-gage shotgun, perhaps the following, sad and tragic event might have been avoided. I've never quite gotten over the guilt of doing good work. This event taught me the merits of being a fuck up. The "accident" was naturally all my fault. This was a very heavy burden for a young teenagers growing up in rural Vermont.

The group of marksmen assembled today at the strip of grass known as the Manchester Airport was all extremely good shots; some of them champion shooters. At this time in my life, I was able to run 96 birds out of a hundred. Charlie and Norbert were good for 100 out of 100 with great consistency. The problem with consistency is that it gets real boring. Throw the bird.

[42]

Much like a Frisbee, the bird floats up into the air. You shoot. The bird disintegrates into a cloud of black dust. You throw another bird. Etc. Etc.

We had gone to gun clubs that had real skeet shooting. By that I mean they had towers that automatically threw out the clay birds. The course is laid out in a half circle with a low tower on your right and a high tower on your left. Station 1 begins with your back to the high tower. Birds are released with great speed from both towers. You smoke the bird coming at you from the low tower first and then pick up the bird coming over your head on its way away from you. Then you smoke that one. Then you move a few paces to your right and do it again. You keep going to station #7 where the low tower is on your immediate right (you never stand with your back to the low tower, duh, because the bird would hit you in the head; hence the name "Low Tower").

Station #8 is where things get exciting. You are equidistant between the two towers, which are roughly 50 yards apart. That may sound like a lot, but when you have birds coming at you from two different directions 180 degrees from each other let it suffice to say that for that split second of your life you are one busy boy. The speed of the bird's flight forces you to slow everything down. What the spectators see as a hair trigger you see as a finger made of lead that is taking forever and a day to squeeze the metal trigger. Bang Bang. Just like that and two birds are reduced to dust. You don't even realize you've hit them both until the barrel of your gun is on its way down towards the ground.

Here we are all in a line facing east looking down the 3,000 foot runway. Right in the middle of the line was Charlie. In Charlie's right hand, instead of a 12-gage shotgun, was a hand-held skeet thrower. Charlie had agreed to start off throwing. We would all always take a turn at throwing, which sometimes could prove to be as much if not more exciting than actually shooting. This was one of those times.

Bird after bird lobed out into the air; coasting beautifully against the cobalt blue Vermont summer sky. That bird was lucky if it made it out 50 feet before at least a half-dozen men all fired within a nanosecond of each other. I never did stop to calculate how many ounces of lead hit one bird simultaneously, but I'm sure that I could have using the scale in the basement.

Before long, boredom set in. I mean, this really was too easy for a group of guys who were used to shooting birds coming at you from every direction and at twice the speed. It was Charlie who came up with the idea that would end up ruining his day and nearly his life.

"How about we try something different" he said. This could only spell trouble. Breaking out of the norm was something the Buchmayr Boys were well accustomed to. The rest of us were OK with the norm.

"What's your idea?" someone said.

"How about if I walk out there (pointing down the airstrip) and throw birds at you guys just like what happens at station #8 with the low tower?"

What could possibly go wrong? All of the shooters standing in the straight line looked at each other with a degree of befuddlement mixed with amusement. We were, after all, good sports and hated to piss on one's good idea. In the back of my head, I was trying to come to grips with the fact that it would be nearly impossible NOT to shoot Charlie. As I was wondering just how we were going to go about implementing this fabulous idea, Charlie spoke.

"Now listen, I'm going to throw this bird low, just like the low tower, and it should soar right over your heads.

Uh huh.

"If I throw it too low and it doesn't rise up like it should then don't shoot." he said.

Well, that seemed to make sense on some level. I couldn't help but wonder if maybe he should try one or two practice throws; you know, just to warm up a bit, but I was the youngest one there and I would refer you back to the part about listening versus talking. This was one of those listening times. I figured if everyone else was cool with this hair-brained idea, I was, too. I was already conjuring up what I would tell the cops. "It was his idea, officer."

Sure enough, Charlie marched right on out onto the runway. I'm not sure just how far away he ended up from us, but I can assure you it wasn't far enough. I was already having a bad feeling about all this. Fortunately, I possess the inner will to push things like bad feelings back into the dark hole where they belong. All these feelings ever do is to prohibit you from having some of life's greatest experiences.

Charlie stopped and faced the line of shooter friends; or so he thought were his friends. He pushed a clay pigeon into the Y shaped slot secured to a heavy duty spring, which was secured to a hardwood handle.

"You ready?" he shouted. It seemed odd that he would have felt compelled to ask. Everyone facing was a hair-trigger shooter with loaded 12-gage shotguns just dying to touch off a round.

"OK, remember what I said. If it's too low, don't shoot." he hollered.

Uh huh.

He pulled back his arm stretching out the shoulder that years later he would dislocate in one of many of his car accidents and not unlike Sandy Kovach, launching one from the pitcher's mound. Charlie let this bird fly with every ounce of strength he had.

The good news is that the bird came at us fast and straight. The bad news was that when I pulled my gun up to shoot I saw the bird blocking out Charlie's perfect smile. Miraculously, I was able to continue on with my swing forcing the barrel of my gun to rise almost vertically straight up in the air. My mind was racing. Whew, that was clos......BANG.

By the time the one shot went off Charlie, never accused of being anybody's fool, had already dropped the skeet thrower, covered his head with both arms and began turning his back on what used to be his friends.

The heads of those in the line were whipping left and right to see who the hell had fired. I mean, jeez, everyone had to see that the bird was about five feet; one inch off the ground. There stood Siggy with literally the smoking gun. Charlie seemed to have instinctively known it was Sig because he came running with such determination and fury that it was pretty obvious that the thrower that he had tossed to the ground but now picked back up was destined to be sunk right into Sig's skull.

After all these years I've often wondered if Sig shot because he just couldn't stand passing up the bird (highly likely and excusable) or was it because he was the fraternal twin? Notice Norbert didn't take the shot. They might've been fighting in the womb and had never yet settled that score. Who knows? All I knew at this moment in time, that was already dragging out into about five eternities, was that Sig Buchmayr shot his brother in the ass and was about to pay for it with his life, which didn't seem at all fair; but then again I wasn't the one with a butt full of #9 bird shot.

Charlie got about 20 feet away. He looked like one of those crazed Indians in the old "B" movies flailing away with a tomahawk, except his tomahawk wasn't quite as sharp, which meant that it might take more than one blow to split open Sig's head. At or around 20 feet out Norbert stepped out in front of Sig, raised his gun and aimed it right at Charlie's nose.

"Stop right there." he commanded.

Always the one to use good judgment under fire (no pun intended), Charlie stopped dead in his tracks. He knew his brother pretty well and was about 100% confident that Norbert would blow his head off.

"He fucking shot me!" Charlie screamed loud enough that I'm sure they heard it at the Equinox Hotel which would close down a year later (not because of anything we did).

"If you had been up here, you would've taken the shot, too. You know you would", Norbert stated calmly while not letting up on the shotgun for one second. We always hated when Norbert would interject logic into a somewhat heightened anxiety situation. He made everyone stop and think for a minute. It was exasperating.

"Turn around. Let's take a look." Norbert requested. Charlie turned around. Already red dots of blood were appearing on the back side of his chinos. Some of the pellets had raked up his back and I seem to recall that one might have pierced his ear.

Norbert assessed the situation and told everyone to load up the Rover as we now had to go back to the house and deal with the situation. "Don't worry about picking up the spent shells. Bobby can come back up later and get them." Happy to.

The ride in the rigid Rover down the bumpy, dirt road from the airport had be nearly as, if not more, painful than the initial shooting. If it hurt, no one in the Rover knew it because Charlie was not about to let on that he was in any pain. Hell, he looked like we might be on our way out for breakfast.

We arrived at the little red house, unloaded the truck, and got Charlie inside. As Charlie was unbuckling his pants, someone reached under the counter and pulled out a bottle of Blackberry Brandy. For those of you unaccustomed to things like getting shot in the butt or getting your thumb squashed between two pieces of firewood (see "How to Survive the Recession – A Vermont Perspective for more on squashed thumbs), then you might not fully appreciate the medicinal value of Blackberry Brandy. When things go awry, there's no other better medicine; notwithstanding the uncontrollable vomiting that occurs later on.

The bottle was opened as the pants came down. Whoa baby, a butt full of pellets is one ugly site. Where to begin? Norbert was there with one pair of tweezers and someone else, perhaps Tony but I couldn't swear to it, was there with another pair. Charlie had a firm grip on the bottle, which was unfortunate because the rest of us could've used a pull or two, but no one had the balls to take the bottle away from Charlie especially in his, shall we say, compromised state.

Pluck, pluck, pluck. What a way to spend a glorious summer day pulling #9 bird shot out of your friend's ass. There was an apology offered that help take out some of the sting. However, the apology was quickly followed with statements stating the obvious, like, "Jeez, Charlie, that was the dumbest fucking idea you've ever had."

Naturally, Charlie got a little defensive and responded saying, "I told you not to shoot if the goddamn bird was too low you asshole.", or something along those lines. You get the picture. After a few hours, a bottle of Blackberry Brandy, and an accommodating bottle of iodine, Charlie was as good as new. Well, notwithstanding the nasty, uncontrollable vomiting that occurs after drinking a bottle of Blackberry Brandy. Within a matter of hours, he was able to sit down again presumably because he was numb from head to toe.

As we've all come to learn, time is the healer of all wounds and this event was no exception. Charlie recovered nicely. To look at him a few days later, you would have had no idea he had been shot in the ass. Well, you might have noticed that he did favor one side of the bar stool over the other, but still, it would've taken a pretty keen eye.

Charlie ended up not killing Siggy. I ended up going back up to the scene of the crime and retrieving all of the spent shells. I knew right where we had all been standing by the fact that one area was littered with the spent, red casings. I knew right where I had been standing and looked out over the airstrip where hours ago I, too had almost pulled the trigger and loaded up Charlie's butt with #9 bird shot. I knew right where Sig had been standing, too. I picked up the shells. One of these shells had been responsible for what some might see as a terrible event. We saw it more like a family bonding experience.

A couple of days later I was back in the basement taking a spent shell out of the box and placing it into the reloading machine. I stared at the first empty bullet for a few seconds and wondered to myself if maybe I should not fill this one with #9 bird shot.

It should be noted that Charlie did not shoot his brother in an act of retaliation. Frankly, it is believed that after consuming a bottle of Blackberry Brandy that Charlie may very well have forgotten about the entire incident. Although they constantly argued about everything imaginable, it's safe to say that the two brothers recovered quite nicely. In the end, one learned never to throw low, the other to aim high. It all worked out.

[49]

CHAPTER 5

Watch Where You're Spittin'

After being around for sixty-three years, I can say with a great deal of confidence that it's not easy dying of cancer. I don't care who you are, it's a bitch of a way to go. I would much prefer the method of having my heart explode while playing the best harmonica solo of all time before a sellout crowd of passionate Blues lovers. I guess I don't get to call that one.

Some people handle the news of a diagnosis differently than others. Some, understandably, freak out while others seem to take the news in stride. It's hard telling why this is other than perhaps that people are different. There are no two the same. Different people do things differently (write that down, because you won't get information like this just anywhere).

Roger Secoy was the guy from whom I purchased my firewood. I'd known Roger forever as some guy around town, but never really knew him until I started buying firewood from him. You get to know a lot about a man when you buy firewood from him, especially if he's willing to talk at all. Some folks move up here to Vermont, locate a guy that sells firewood, place an order and may very well not have a conversation more in depth than the one described in a previous chapter. Most Vermonters aren't all that wordy so it's left up to you to figure out just what the hell is going on inside their heads.

There is most likely a very good reason for this curtailed desire to divulge much information. First and foremost, the average Vermonter is terrified that they may have a slip of the tongue and unintentionally disclose the location of the best fishing hole in the state. They know that doing so leaves one with very few options; the best being Hari-kari, and no you don't get to use a sharp knife. You have to grind away for a while just to remind yourself in your final moments what a dumbass you were for giving up that hole.

Although the following slogan is not recited daily in our classrooms around the state, it should be. It is taught to most Vermonters at a very young age and accommodated by a slap upside the head if ever violated. It goes something like this: "When in public or talking to a stranger, it's best to remain silent and let them wonder if you're an idiot as opposed to opening your mouth and proving it."

Those are damn good words to live by right there. I'm sure Roger learned this as a youngster and repeated it often. He didn't need to, mind you, as he was one smart cookie but you'd never know from talking with him. You had to work through it. Some of my first conversations with Roger went something like this:

"How you doing?"

"I'm dying"

"Of what?"

"Cancer"

"You sell firewood?"

"Yup"

"You wanna sell me some?"

"I guess"

And from this insightful, if not overly verbose introduction, began a friendship that lasted right up until he died. Roger had a very weird kind of cancer. He had tumors in his legs that would grow to weigh as much as twenty pounds. He was a regular at the Dartmouth Medical Center Cancer Clinic in Hanover, New Hampshire. They were able to stave off the inevitable for about a decade and half, which seemed pretty remarkable, even to Roger.

Understand that I didn't start right off asking him about his cancer. That would've been impolite. You let Vermonters offer up information on their own terms. "How do you get them to define their own terms?" you ask. You could start by buying their firewood.

has to cut down a tree. That'll warm you up right there. Then drag it out of the forest and cut A week or so later and after a load or two had been delivered, Roger and I were standing around in my driveway behind my woodshed. I looked at him and said, "You in any pain?"

"Nope. I have some help loading the truck and as you can see it's a dump truck. It don't hurt much working this lever."

I didn't say anything. Just stood there looking at him.

"Oh, you mean the cancer? Yeah. Some."

"You taking anything for the pain?" I asked taking great pains not to get into a full-fledged conversation.

"Used to, but it made me sick. Don't like taking drugs much; only if I have to." He said.

"So, you just grunt through it?"

"When it gets real bad, I go up to the brook on Toll Gate Road. You know it?"

I nod that I do.

"I make sure no one's around; strip down and then lay down in the brook for a while."

I go numb just thinking about this.

"How long you lay there for?"

"Til I can't stand it. 45 minutes; sometimes an hour."

Think about this for a minute, folks. I don't know how much time you've spent wallowing around in Vermont brooks, but let me assure you that they are SOME GODDAMN COLD. If you can get in one at all, you're tough. You go numb in a minute or so. Lying in a Vermont brook for nearly an hour is, shall we say in a word, insane. I can fathom how much pain you'd have to be in to cause you to lay down in the Toll Gate Brook, but let's agree that it'd have to be pretty substantial.

"That work?" I asked

"Pretty much." He replied.

Some people run right over to their doctor to get a prescription for some sort of pain killer. Roger found his own, more natural method of dealing with pain. He probably figured if it was good enough for the Indians that used to live around here it was probably good enough for him. It worked better and was better for him.

I always had Roger deliver the next season's firewood in the spring, long before I was ever planning on burning it, for two reasons. First, it would give the wood more than enough time to dry inside my shed over the hot summer months so that when the heating season began, I'd be burning real nice dry wood. The second reason is a little more obscure. If one heats their home solely on wood for over three decades, they develop a healthy respect for their fuel. You come to understand what goes into it. Someone it up. Those are two more opportunities to get warm. Then it must be split and laid out in a way that it'll dry out some. There's another warming event. Now you have to load the wood in a delivery truck, which causes the handler to heat up once again. Now, dumping the load is not very exhausting, but in my later years I took to having my wood stacked inside the shed. I did this for two reasons; I got real tired of stacking wood in my shed, and two, I didn't want to deprive Roger's crew of yet another heating opportunity. All in all, one stick of wood will provide heat on about seven separate occasions. You don't get nearly this much heat out of gas or oil and neither of those two sources is renewable.

There is no better feeling in the world than having a shed full of firewood by the end of May. You can go out to your woodshed every day and just look at it. It's a whole lot better than money in the bank and heats better than burning dollar bills in a woodstove. Having a shed full of wood provides its owners with a sense of security and allows them to believe that if the shit hits the fan, at least they won't freeze to death come next winter. Here in Vermont, we tend to live season to season. Getting through winter is the tough one and if there's even a remote chance of freezing to death, it makes it real hard to sleep at night.

The prospects of death never did seem to interfere with Roger's outlook on life. Later that summer, around August, I was outdoors working when I heard a truck coming up my long driveway. I could tell it was Roger right away. His red truck, like its driver, had seen better days. The fenders seemed to flap as he went down the road. Every once in a while, the pistons used to raise the dump body to dump out the wood, would burst which would often times lead to a calamity. Everything is fixable so there was never any need to worry.

"What on earth is Roger doing coming up my driveway in the middle of August? I got all my wood in. I paid him. I shouldn't be seeing him until late next winter." I thought to myself.

Sure enough, there was Roger and his big beautiful Rottweiler, Dekon, who went everywhere with him. He stopped in my driveway. He never made any attempt to actually park the truck anywhere, nor did he make any effort to get out. He just sat there with his window down and his arm hanging out the truck door. His baseball hat sat firmly on his head. Dekon leaned forward to get a good look at me and made a quick decision that I was probably harmless. I was grateful. Of course, I made no attempt to make direct eye contact with the dog. That's never a good idea.

I walked over to the truck and stood there for an awkwardly long time just trying to figure out why he was here.

"What's up?" I asked.

"Just checkin' on your wood." He said with a bit, just a slight bit, of a grin.

"Well, it's about 88 degrees today so I'm not going through it like I will be in a few months" I said using way more words than I should have in this situation, but I was nervous.

"I'd say I'm still pretty much set with wood. What else is going on?"

Sometimes all you need to do is to have a sixth sense about things. There was a second reason why Roger was in my yard and to discover what that was one had to be exercise extreme caution for fear of having him clam right up.

"I'm drivin' newbies" he said.

For a guy who doesn't say much, he sure is intriguing. What the hell was a newbie? Driving what? That truck? Heaven forbid. Has Roger's mind finally gone numb from lying in the Toll Gate Brook? A few words left plenty of questions. I decided to take the cautious approach.

"Where to?"

"Dartmouth"

"Hmm, OK"

"You have any idea how terrifying it is for a newbie?"

I wasn't sure I knew yet what a newbie was, but I feared being seen as an idiot by my wood guy just for asking.

"No"

"There's no worse feeling in the world than the first time your doctor tells you got cancer. It's terrifying."

I opted to just stand there and let my eyes tell him that I believed what he was saying.

"You know the only thing worse than getting' diagnosed?"

I couldn't imagine that there could be anything worse.

"Nope."

"Going over to Dartmouth for the first time. You ever been there?"

Turned out I had once. It's a large complex. I told him that I had once a long time ago.

"Can you imagine how it feels to know you've got cancer and then drive over there and park your car and try to figure out where you're going and do that all by yourself?"

I felt a wave of nausea come over me.

"I can't" I said sheepishly.

"If you've never done this then you just can't. I told the people at the hospital that I'd be willing to drive the newbies, that's what I call people just diagnosed, over to the hospital and take them where they needed to go. Everyone over there knows me, because I've had 14 surgeries so far. I have a lot of friends there. It ain't so bad once you get over the fear." He said.

"You driving people from this area over there?"

"Yup."

One thing about cancer is that it doesn't discriminate. Rich people and poor people alike get cancer. Just because you're rich doesn't mean that you have any less fear than someone who's poor. Most likely, you have more fear because you have a lot more to lose. The poor don't have a whole lot to lose and although I'm sure they're in no hurry to leave, they might be thinking that moving on might be a better deal than what they have going on here. Either way, there's plenty of fear to be had.

I couldn't help to wonder just how Rodger was transporting these folks. I guess his dump truck would make it there and back, but I wouldn't wager a lot of money on it. Then there was the prospect of Roger driving someone's Mercedes 550 SL. At any given time, Rodger had somewhere between some and plenty of grease on his pants. He also chewed. I've never been a big fan of chewing. I did try it as a kid, but near puked the first time. I couldn't see much point in it. I guess the idea is to avoid lung cancer.

If you're a chewer, you're by default a spitter. You best not be swallowing that brown spooge that the tobacco creates when mixed with your saliva. You have to spit it out. Some guys spit in an old soda can. Some spit on the ground, but they all spit.

The entire time I had been talking with Rodger, he had been spitting on the floor of his truck. Now, when your wood guy and your friend is spitting on the floor of his own truck, the last thing you ever want to say is something like, "What a fucking pig. I can't believe you're spiting that shit on the floor of your own truck. That's fucking disgusting."

I mean, you CAN say that, but I'll bet the price of your wood will go up next year. Instead you have to be a little more careful; more subtle. I took the careful, subtle approach.

"You takin' 'em over in your truck?"

I get a very disapproving look.

Looking through squinting eyes he said, "Jesus, no."

Puzzled I asked, "How you getting them there?"

"We take their car. Some of the people from over this way that become newbies have some pretty nice cars, too."

Naturally, this sets my mind racing. It's tough to visualize Rodger behind the wheel of the Mercedes 550 SL. It even harder to imagine the poor guy who has to do the detailing and clean up three cups of slimy spooge on the floor upon their return from New Hampshire.

Looking for the shock value I looked right into Rodger's eyes and asked, "You spit on the floor of their cars, too?"

Like most members of his family, Rodger is a bit intimidating. He had a stare that would make most people shit their pants on the spot. If you knew Rodger real well, you might be able to hold it for a minute or two. He was the nicest, kindest guy in the world, but he looked like he could and would kill you at the drop of a hat. I was thinking that maybe that last question had crossed the line.

After a long time of staring at each other, Rodger slowly raised his arm off the truck door where it had been resting. He extended it straight out. I knew he wasn't going to hit me as his arm and hand were moving so slowly. When his arm was fully extended, using his index finger, he pointed straight down. He never said a word. He just pointed.

I gave him a questioning, puzzled look, but didn't say anything. He raised his arm up in the air and then, with what I would describe as with great exuberance, jammed his finger downward cutting through the hot August air. He was answering my question, but I was too stupid to get it.

I backed up about two paces and looked down. At that precise moment Rodger let a pretty big spit loose. I saw it leave his mouth and then instantly appear in the brown puddle now in my driveway. It was about the size of a soccer ball. I looked up at Rodger and he was just grinning away.

I told him I thought it was incredibly kind of him to take the time out of his workday to drive people to Dartmouth just to help them overcome their fear of the place.

In the end Rodger never did recover from his two decades long battle with the weirdest cancer in the world. What he did do though, was to show me that he was a much different person than I ever thought him to be. Underneath the gruff surface of a guy who appeared to be one of the low people, was a very intelligent and caring man.

As I mentioned, Rodger had a way about him. He'd never come right out and say what it was he was going to be talking about.

For instance, he pulled into my driveway one day and again just parked randomly wherever he happened to stop.

"You ever seen any fisher cats up this way?" he asked.

Right out of the freakin' blue. Why on earth would this guy drive all the way up to my place just to ask me if I've ever seen a fisher cat; one of the hardest cats in the world to actually lay your eyes on in the woods? You stand a better chance of finding the Hope Diamond in the organic bananas section at your local supermarket than seeing a fisher cat, ever.

"Nope. Never seen one." I said throwing caution to the wind using four words when I could've answered his question with only one. I stopped to think for a minute and went off practically reciting the Gettysburg Address.

"Didn't know we had fisher cats around here." I said.

"I took six off this hill. My buddy got three more." he said as I stood there astonished.

"WHAT?"

"Yeah, we got a call from the game warden asking us to trap 'em out of here as they were becoming a downright nuisance up here." he said.

How the hell could an animal, that I've never seen before but would give my eye tooth to see, be so plentiful in my neighborhood that they've become a nuisance and have to be trapped? He had to be pulling my leg (no pun intended).

"Why'd the warden call you?"

"Your neighbor on the road up above you had an incident."

This didn't sound good.

"Turned out the daughter opened the door to let their cat out at around 7:30 in the morning. The cat sauntered out on the front step, stood there for a second or two and whoosh, that was it. A fisher had come out of nowhere, grabbed the cat right off the step and was gone. Just like that. The kid screamed. The parents freaked and called the cops who, rightfully, said there was nothing they could do and suggested calling the game warden, which they did. The warden, rightfully, said that he's not responsible for events like this and that you should call someone who might be able to trap the scoundrel that got your cat. They called me."

Now, this was about the longest speech I ever heard from Rodger and I sat there riveted, not only at the content, but at learning he could go on this long.

"We, my buddy and I, came up here and looked around. Looked like fisher country to us. We set traps expecting to catch one, maybe two. We were both surprised to get as many cats here as we did. Got a good buck for the pelts, too." he explained.

"So, you're OK with trapping animals? You don't think it's inhumane?" I knew this question would get him, because if you're a trapper (I was once when I was younger), you don't think it's inhumane at all.

"You rather that they over populate to the degree where they snatch some poor kid's cat right off the doorstep? They're a vicious creature and nothing to tangle with."

I didn't take the bait. I knew that he knew that I knew what he was saying was true. I also knew that it was one of the various ways in which Rodger supported himself. Between the two of them, they made $900 trapping these cats; $100 per catch. They were happy. The cat's owners were happy (sort of) and the world kept moving along.

When this exchange of words was over, I stopped to recall that I had had at least two cats disappear over the many years I've

[63]

lived here. It never occurred to me that perhaps they had met their demise at the jaws and claws of a fisher cat, but hearing Rodger describe the (over) population on this hill, I now would not be at all surprised.

It may seem like a crude way to make a living, but it's really not. It's nothing more than part of the cycle. It's been a few years since anyone's trapped fisher cats up this way and I suspect that by now they might be right back in this area. It would be great fun to see one, but inasmuch as I've not seen one in 63 years, I don't expect I'll see one anytime soon.

CHAPTER 6

The Exploding Cow

To quote Buddy Guy, "Look-ah-here".

It is my hope that by now you are beginning to get a handle on how you're going to best survive this Recovery that we are supposed to be in. Yes, pickins appear to be slim for the time being, but better days are ahead. You gotta believe that there is a pot of gold at the end of your somewhat fading rainbow. You're in the perfect place to be able to take full advantage of the Recovery, because you're at rock bottom. Think about it. How the hell do you expect to go up when you're already at the very top? All you do way up there is fall and fall you will. It's just a matter of how far and how hard.

You, you lucky bastard, have beat those guys to it and are now in the toilet. You may be looking around thinking to yourself that the toilet is no place to be as it tends to be full of shit occasionally. That's the kind of thinking that's been holding you back. Your toilet is NOT full of shit ALL THE TIME, only once in a while. So, instead of focusing on those times when your toilet is full of shit, you would be much better off thinking about the times when you're surrounded by cool, clean water. Start thinking this way and you'll be on your way back up in no time.

Speaking of being covered with shit; I would caution you about standing too close to a cow that is about to explode.

Growing up in Vermont did not come without some serious responsibilities. You had all kinds of things for which you were responsible. You had to mow the lawn, help out around the house, and you were expected to help out your neighbor if they needed help. We had a neighbor who needed help.

Actually, he wasn't a neighbor per se. Jim Kelleher lived on Dorset West Rd. in Dorset, Vermont. We lived on Rt. 30. If we shot a rifle straight out our back door (not that we ever would) we'd hit Jimmy's house square on. As long as I could remember, he lived with his mom in the little farmhouse on the rocky farm.

He had a small barn near the house and a dilapidated barn across the street where he kept things like the 3-point plow that I would use many years later to plow the earth in preparation for my first garden on my new house.

Even on a tiny farm like Jim's, there was plenty of stuff that needed doing. During the summer, we might help him hay or mess with the 60 or so cows he had. He knew each and every cow by name. They were his closest friends. There was always something that needed to be painted. When I was around eleven, I found myself on a ladder leaned up against the east side of the small barn; the one that housed the cows and was in respectable condition. In my left hand I held a bucket of barn red (what else, really) paint. In my right hand was a 4-inch brush that I used to slather on the paint. I believe this was my first painting job. Years later I would discover that the only job I would ever be fired from was painting.

You could paint next to Jim for days on end and neither one of you would say a word. I sure as hell was not about to be the one to break the dump truck load of silence that was mounting up between us. Silence is a funny thing. At first it feels a little awkward being about 5 feet away from another person and not speaking; not one word. Then after a while the silence begins to take shape. It becomes heavy like a rock. Even if you felt compelled to say something, you'd think twice about it because you wouldn't want to be the one that broke the chain of silence that adding new links with each passing hour. It almost becomes a contest; a test of wills. You resign yourself to not being the one to speak, ever, no matter what.

OK, so there may be some exceptions to this rule. If you see something that might be life threatening, I think it's fair to look at the other person, shuck your head over to the direction in which the trouble may be occurring, and offer a slight, low grunt or barely audible expression. In times like these, it might be best to avoid using actual words. Let the other person decide whether or not the circumstances require a response that would, in turn, allow you to expand on your grunt.

This might have been one of those times. Turned out it really wasn't, but like I said, I was young and had not yet fully learned the nuances of silence. We were painting away perfectly happy not saying a word, baking in the hot sun. The paint was drying so fast it nearly dried from the time my brush left the bucket to when it touched the clapboards.

One of the downsides to painting barns in the summertime is hornets. We have an overabundance of hornets in this state. Too bad my friend, Rodger, couldn't trap these little creatures. They're everywhere. I was taught at an early age to simply ignore them. Pay them no mind. Don't act like you're afraid of them, because like all animals, they can smell fear.

So here I am, scared to death, throwing fear out much like the participants of the Mardi Gras Parade tossing out beads. Every hornet within 100 miles had to smell my fear because it seemed like there were thousands of them all around us. I refused to let them get to me. I looked over at Jim who was in his own little world just painting away. I don't think he even knew there were hornets all around us.

Jim had worked on this farm, all by himself, for as long as I can remember. He was a soft spoken, gentle man, but he was also as tough as nails. He had the most calloused hands of anyone I had ever known. He had farmer's hands. He was standing on his ladder leaning back a bit to admire his work. He was a pretty good painter. He didn't miss too many spots, not that you could really tell, because we were painting red on red. If you missed a spot this year, you'd be sure to get it in another couple of years.

Jim was holding his paint can in his left hand and his brush in his right. At the same moment that he was admiring his work, a hornet was admiring his right hand. I saw the hornet land right on the palm of his hand holding the brush. Just as I was about to yell out "Jim, there's a hornet on your hand!" Jim looked downward at his hand. I couldn't help it. I broke all the rules and yelled out anyway.

Jim never responded, nor did he move one muscle. He was as still as a cat ready to catch a mouse. Inasmuch as both of his hands were occupied, I couldn't imagine how he was going to swat that hornet. He just stood there. For reasons I can't understand today, after all these years, the hornet picked its butt up high in the air and jammed its stinger straight into Jim's palm. I almost dropped my paint and brush from the pain and it wasn't me who got stung. Jim never blinked. He didn't do anything. Now it could've been the callouses or maybe it was the volumes of beer that he drank every day, who knows? Either way, it didn't faze him in the least.

The hornet, on the other hand, had made a grave error. He had jammed his stinger into the wrong palm. The hornet attempted to pull back and tried to yank its stinger out of Jim's hand. He pulled and pulled to no avail. Finally, he gave one last huge effort and yanked away. The stinger didn't budge, but the tail end of the hornet separated from the rest of its body. One thousand one, one thousand two, one thousand three..... flop. The hornet fell right over and lay dead in the palm of Jim's right hand. Jim looked at the hornet, then looked at me. He moved his head forward, inhaled and blew lungs full of air at the remains of the hornet, which promptly flew through the air and landed gracefully in my paint bucket.

Jim went back to painting without saying a word. He never bothered to remove the stinger because there was no bother from the stinger. I went back to painting, too.

Jim had a pronounced limp. Years later, I learned that it was from a really bad car accident that he had. I never knew him to drive a car. Whenever he needed to go into town, Manchester or Dorset as there was never any other place he needed to go, he would take his John Deere tractor; the one with the bucket on

[69]

the front and sometimes a backhoe like bucket on the back. Jim had the troubles it seemed. He liked his beer and kept to himself, but one could tell he was holding a lot in. It didn't make him any less of a man or a good friend. He just never said much. He ran his little farm and minded his own business. It would have been fun to have known him when he was younger and presumably a little wilder.

The limp bothered him some, not that he'd ever say anything about it, but it didn't get in his way. He got done what needed getting done. A couple of days after a terrific Vermont thunderstorm there was something that needed doing.

Every morning Jim would let the cows out of the barn and let them wander up to The Flats. The Flats were just that; a very flat piece of land that was a ways up the hill behind the farm. It was a great spot where neighborhood kids would go hang out in the summertime.

Every night you could hear Jim calling his cows; even from our house which was well across the west branch of the Battenkill River. On cue, the cows would begin their decent zigzagging down the hill and into the barn. On this day there was a problem; Jim was one cow short. It was too late to go look for her. That would have to wait until the next day.

I arrived at the farm the next morning. Jim had already been up for lord knows how long. The cows were gone, presumably up to The Flats, or at least I was hoping so. I said good morning to Jim. He grunted something back that sounded nothing like good morning and I interpreted as a friendly greeting.

"Better go look for her." he said apparently talking to me, inasmuch as there was no one else within a half-mile. I knew climbing up the mountain with a pronounced limp was going to be tough on Jim. Then I realized that we weren't walking. He fired up the John Deere. Billows of white smoke poured out of the vertical exhaust pipe.

"This thing's only meant for one person, but you're small enough you can sit right here on the fender. Don't fall off." He said.

Now, I was just a kid, maybe around eleven or twelve. That invitation came as a double-edged sword. First of all, it was about the highest honor in the land to be invited up to sit with Jim on his tractor. I couldn't recall any other kid from South Dorset ever receiving this privilege, so immediately I considered myself pretty special.

Then I started pondering on the prospects of falling off the damned thing. If I were to fall off, I would want to make sure that I fell off behind the monster rear tire as opposed to in front of it. Falling behind the tire would likely result in nothing more than a broken collar bone and/or maybe a broken wrist. Falling in front of the tire would be a whole different story. If you're lucky, you'd be crushed instantly and wouldn't have a whole lot of time to dwell on the many years of caked on cow shit on the tire that would be grinding your body to shreds. That would be about the grossest thing in the universe (or at least in the universe of that moment. As I would soon learn, there was at least one thing grosser than this possible death). The kids in the neighborhood would be talking about how I ended up with tread marks from the monster John Deere going right up my body like something out of a Saturday morning cartoon, and they'd laugh up a storm at the gobs of ancient cow shit that filled the tread marks on my head. Nope, no way I was falling off this sucker.

We headed up the old Holton Road, ironically, named after one of the Holtons that lived around here back then. Rachel Holton had married my great, great grandfather, Curtis Stannard, and hence was my great, great grandmother. The green paint on the fender was starting to crack under the extreme pressure of my grip as we began our ascent up the foothills of Mother Myrick.

We entered The Flats from the north side. Sure enough, there were the cows grazing away having the marvelous times that cows have. Oh, I know that you think that cows are dumber than bricks and just stand around in what appears to be utter (versus udder) amazement, but believe me, when you turn your back on these creatures and take your eyes off them they are party animals.

I was busy doing just about everything except looking for a lost cow. I was checking out grey squirrels, chipmunks, scouting for deer, and hanging on for dear life. Jim was much more focused. Suddenly the tractor takes a very sharp turn to the left practically forcing me into Jim's lap. I was mortified that I almost sat in his lap. That might have been worse than falling forward and landing under the monster tire. I doubt anyone actually ever touched Jim and I sure as hell didn't want to be the first.

We turned 90 degrees and were traveling with a sense of urgency across the field mowed down to the height of a putting green thanks to the cows. I've often wondered why we even bother with things like lawn mowers when we have sheep and cows that do a much superior job. Instead of polluting the air with spent gas, they have the extra added benefit of fertilizing the grass they're mowing darned near simultaneously.

Off in the distance, there appeared to be a black and white blob lying on the ground. As we got closer, it was clear that it was the missing cow. Jim backed off on the gas as we got closer. We were right next to the cow; or at least I thought it could be a cow. It more closely resembled a Macy's Day Balloon of a cow. It was huge. No, it was bigger than huge. It's more like a word I would learn much later in life; ginormous. My eyes darted back and forth between the cow-turned-blimp and Jim's face. He was very upset, not that you could tell. He wasn't like bawling or anything, but he was....different. I know this may sound strange and you might not get this, but he was silent. Really silent; not just the normal, everyday kind of silent like where he wouldn't speak for hours on end. I'm talking deep down, inner core silent. If you don't believe that there's a difference between the two, I could understand why. Very few people spend a lot of time with people who don't speak much and then get hit with a traumatic situation that causes them to really clam up tight. This was one of those unique situations.

"We'll have to bury her." Jim said, once again apparently to me, although in fairness he might have been addressing the rest of the herd that had now sauntered over to our end of the field. They looked almost giddy at the thought of something exciting happening out of the routine of their normal days of total and absolute boredom.

I thought it might make more sense to simply let the crows feast away on the carcass for the next three or four years, but Jim had different plans. He turned the John Deere around 180 degrees and, using the backhoe, began digging a hole right next to the recently deceased cow. Just before he started digging, I did about the bravest thing I've ever done. I opted to speak and ask Jim a question.

"Why is she so big, Jim?"

"Hit by lightning. Don't happen often, but it does happen."

I mentally made a note to dive head first in front of the monster tire on the John Deere before I would ever be hit by lightning. The kids in the neighborhood would need a pair of vice grips clamped on the end of their dicks to keep from peeing their pants because they'd be laughing so hard at seeing me look like someone had taken an air hose, stuffed it up my butt, and turned it on full blast. No sir, I made my mind up right then and there that I was never going to be hit by lightning. Uh uh. No way.

Jim was digging away. I was standing on the opposite side of the ever increasingly large hole from the cow. I couldn't take my eyes off this poor creature who just a day ago was partying like it was 1999 with her friends up on The Flats. But she ain't partyin' today. Nope, she was deader than a hammer and blown up like the biggest black and white cow balloon you've ever seen.

In short order, Jim had dug an oversized grave for an oversized cow. He backed off the throttle and sat there for a minute, apparently contemplating what to do next. He backed up the John Deere and turned it around so that the bucket would now be the tool of choice to push the once wild and crazy party cow into the freshly dug hole. This seemed like a very logical thing to do since the creature must've weighed hundreds of pounds; although she looked like she weighed thousands.

"Stand back a bit." he said. This was very good advice. It turned out to be a real shame that he didn't define "a bit". I took a step or two backwards away from the grave. As I would soon learn I should've taken about one hundred to two hundred steps backwards.

With amazement and wonderment I watched as Jim carefully positioned the tractor's bucket right behind the cow and prepared to push her into her final resting place. He probably moved the cow all of an inch when without any notice – KABANG.

I never knew what hit me. All I knew was I was having trouble seeing and thought that somehow I, too, had been hit by lightning. I was struggling with this as there wasn't a cloud in the sky. How could I have been hit by lightning on such a beautiful da….. OH MY GOD, what's that smell.

A lot of things happen simultaneously when a cow explodes. It's probably not unlike when a terrorist sets off a car bomb; something totally unheard of in the early '60s. First, there is the element of surprise. You hear an explosion, or in my case, just a dull thud/popping noise. Then something happens to you. In the case of a car bomb you're most likely dead you lucky bastard. In the case of an exploding cow, the side of you facing the cow is completely and thoroughly covered with whatever it is that resides inside of a cow; with one minor (or maybe not so minor) exception. Whatever was inside the cow had been fermenting for a day or so. I'm not saying that this made all that much difference, because even if the insides of this cow had been in tip top shape this sordid event would still have been plenty disgusting.

Next comes the state of denial. No fucking way am I standing up here on The Flats with Jim and the rest of the audience (the other cows who were no doubt by now struggling with the mixed of emotions of sadness at having lost one of their own and utter hysteria about watching a young boy nearly completely covered with exploding cow guts. NO, this CANNOT be happening.

Then there is the final, depressing stage of acquiescence. Man, this stage really does suck. You come to grips with your new reality, which is not a pretty reality; oh boy, not pretty at all. You really are completely covered with guts from a cow that just exploded. OK, so I may be exaggerating here. In fairness, the back side of my body was clean as a whistle. It was only the front of me that was covered, but you can see how I might have easily come to believe that I was completely covered.

"You OK?" Jim asked.

Am I OK? No, I am not fucking OK. I'm standing here on The Flats with 59 cows staring at me with those big round black eyes that don't give anything away (don't ever play poker with one of these things. You'll lose your shirt. They always look like they're bluffing, but they're not). No, I am ten thousand light years away from being OK!!!

"Yeah, I'm OK." I said.

Jim pushed what was left of the cow into the hole and covered her up while I just stood there stinking to high heaven and wondering how my skin would feel after pouring about 500

[75]

gallons of chlorine bleach all over myself for the next, oh I don't know, six or eight months maybe. I was also wondering if whether or not Jim was ever going to share this disgusting-times-ten event with another human being. I was wondering if I should not take that chance and just bury Jim along with his cow. No, that wouldn't work as he was much stronger than me. I couldn't take him; no way. Then I thought that the only honorable solution would be to bury ME with the cow. What the hell? In an instant, I had become one with this creature. It would be like hari-kari or something. Just go down with the cow ship, captain.

The burial was finished when Jim said, "I think you should get in the bucket."

Perfect, he really was going to bury me with the cow. No one would ever have to know. The kids in the neighborhood would never have to clamp vice grips on their collective penises to keep from laughing at me for 100 eternities because the entire sad story was going to stay right here on The Flats.

Not so lucky. I got into the bucket on the front of the tractor because there was no way in God's green earth that Jim was going to have some kid covered in stinking, fermented cow guts sitting on the nice fender of his John Deere tractor. I couldn't blame him.

The ride back down the mountain was bumpy. The solid steel container in which I found myself not only did nothing to absorb the bumps, but instead seemed to amplify every one of them. I was bouncing around banging myself on the hardened steel bucket thinking that it served me right. From that day forward, if anyone ever told me that I should stand back a bit, you can be assured that I knew full well just what "a bit" meant. You'd be lucky if you could ever find me again.

We made it back down to the farm. Jim said, "You might want to hose yourself off before you head home. I think we've had enough for today."

For today? Jesus, I had had about enough forever. I hosed myself off with the freezing cold spring water that ran out of the hose. It felt good. I numbed up real well, but it did little to eliminate the stench, which if the circumstances are just right, I can still smell today. That odor has filled the room as this is being written.

Time moved on and I did recover from this event. I got home. Removed my clothes and tossed them straight into the garbage can in the garage. I walked naked from the garage to the house. Well, not exactly naked as I was living in a shroud of cow gut stink. I walked right past my mom who looked at me as though I was a zombie or something. That is until the smell caught up to her nose.

"What's that awful smell?" she asked.

I kept walking straight to the shower where I spent about the next hour of my life contemplating just how far away "a bit" really is while scrubbing away with a bar of LifeBoy Soap..

If you can live through a cow exploding then Surviving a Recession should be a piece of cake.

CHAPTER 7

Background Check

This might be a good time for a little history lesson. For those of you who are too busy fighting off the squirrels for a few beechnuts, you may be interested in knowing that the Recession that began in 2007 under the then watchful eye of George W. Bush, has ended. Actually, it ended quite some time ago; somewhere around March of 2009.

"Say what?" you say. You're still sleeping in a van down by the river and running around picking shit with chickens just to stay alive so perhaps you have not had much time to pay attention to the good times. Had you not lost everything you owned, you'd be doing great right now.

In your current state, this may come of little solace to you but listen to this news from CNN Money: From 2007 to 2009, the S&P 500 lost more than half of its value. HALF! Jeez, that's a lot. It dropped from 1,500 down to only 676.5! Of course, in your case, you lost 100% which really had to hurt but still the 1% of the richest people in the country had to suffer; OK, be inconvenienced by losing half of their holdings.

That's the bad news. The good news is that since 2009 stocks have soared! Not only have they recouped their losses, but they are now reaching record highs. The S&P is back up to 1,630.7!! Aren't you just thrilled? Things are getting better!

Oh, look at you sitting there on your nearly worn out, old cardboard box, the same one that you flip over at night and use for shelter, feeling sorry for yourself. You should stand up, pin your shoulders back, and be thoroughly proud of yourself that you came up with the idea of using the same cardboard box for both your chair AND your housing. Hell, you're damn near on your way to the road to Recovery.

OK, so we lost 8.8 million jobs. Don't your feel better now? Haven't you ever heard of the old phrase, "Misery loves company?" Remember, you are not alone. Unlike those poor rich people who had to suffer alone, and in sheer terror, as they watched their holdings decrease by HALF, you, you ungrateful son-of-a-bitch, at least had 8.8 million people right there along with you. To listen to you, one would think that you were the only person jumping off the Titanic and into the freezing Artic waters. Just suck it up, would you please?

Take a good look at how things have bounced right back since 2007. Well, OK, "bounce" might be too strong a word. Let's say stumbled back like Tiny Tim after Scrooge kicked his crutch out from underneath him. Sure we lost 8.8 million jobs but we've gained back 6.2 million leaving a tiny employment deficit of only 2.6 million. Oh, ye of the "Glass Half Full" mentality. Simply because you so happen to be one of those 2.6 million people staving off wild dogs in hopes of being able to consume the remains of that dead squirrel on the side of the road, doesn't mean things are bad for everyone, does it? You might be better off offering a little sympathy to those who had to endure the trauma of almost being poor.

Ya know, there's a big difference between being poor and almost being poor. You know that, right? Being poor, you have the advantage of knowing that you have somewhere between extremely little and no hope. You're down there, baby. And those moderately helpful government programs that allow you eat at least once every other day are being cut by politicians who feel very strongly that those in the upper tax brackets need some help.

Think about it. The poor are used to being poor. They don't know of anything else but being poor. They're used to being poor by now so losing money that they never had is hardly an inconvenience. There should be a study done to show the nominal impact the Recession had on the mega-poor. Don't get any hair-brained ideas that the study should be funded by additional taxes on the rich. The study should be paid for out of reductions from useless programs like food stamps and Medicare. The poor, as we have just stated, are already poor and won't miss money they don't have. Attempting to extract

[81]

additional funds from the 1% would do nothing more than add to their stress and insecurity. How could you possibly live with yourself if you put these poor (i.e., rich) people through this again?

Look, even the disposable income per capita increased from 2009 to 2013. I hope you're sitting down here, because this good news might cause you to get a little light-headed and I wouldn't want you to fall face first on the floor, thus making that awful splotching sound that a face makes falling from any distance.

Yes, from October 2009 to April of 2013, disposable income increased from $32,000 to $33,000. What the hell did you do with all that extra income you received over the past four years? Knowing you, you probably just pissed it away on Franco American Spaghetti for the kids. I can hear you now pooh poohing the fact that you only got an extra grand. This is very short-sighted thinking and probably the root cause of why you're in the crapper. You need to look at things as others might look at them. The 1% may very well not have recovered all of their losses, yet your disposable income increased. Therefore, one could make the compelling argument that you are WAY better off. See how easy this is to shoulder a little guilt?

Yes, there are some other slightly disturbing statistics that I'm sure you're going to exploit given the chance. Fortunately, no one is listening to you drone on about your petty problems. Were they to bother to listen to you, they would hear the blah, blah, blah of how tough you have it. Look, things are getting better and the last thing this Recovery needs is you sitting around moanin' and groanin' about how shitty your life's going. No one really cares, OK?

Hell, you're practically out of the woods. Remember how we got to where we are? You went right out there and bought a monster house that everyone, including you, knew you couldn't afford. Sure, your friendly banker told you not to worry that you didn't make a whole lot of money. He said you didn't need a lot of money to buy this house because there's no money down and your credit is great! Being the naïve fool you are, you thought Mr. Friendly Banker was looking out for you and your interests (mistake number one). It turned out, in your wildest dreams, you couldn't afford the house and you racked up a load of debt that you could never shovel your way out of.

Since then, however, the household debt per capita has decreased from $53,000 down to a paltry $46,000. Gosh, people today are darn near debt free. That must be where that extra grand went; to paying off the debt that they created (with a little help from Capital One and all the other credit cards you once got in the daily mail).

Yessir there, Ray Charles, things are on their way up, but you're just too blind to see. What you need is a paradigm shift. You need to take off those opaque sunglasses and grab yourself a pair of rose colored glasses. You need to get in line. Shape up, Jack. Stop feeling sorry for yourself. Pull yourself up by your bootstraps. Stop looking for the government handout, because that hand is being severed at the wrist. You gotta cut the line to your water-laden skiff to keep yourself from drowning. The short story is that you've got work to do. And while you're doing it, show a little compassion for others.

When you're standing on the corner beggin' for a dollar from a guy who just stepped out of that brand new Rolls Royce and gives you a look like you might be in the same league as something that was once stuck to the bottom of his shoe that he subsequently had burned, stop and think about someone other than yourself for a change. Yes, you would be so much better off if you could understand that not too long ago, that poor man was pacing the floors at 2:00 am contemplating a new life; a life that would no longer be worth $900 million but only $450 million. Show a little understanding and your life would be so much better off.

Depending on who you talk to, there are poor people in America, (in theory at least) the richest nation in the world. In your spare time, you might wonder how the richest nation could have any poor. This is probably why you're poor.

According to the US Census Bureau, in 2012 the poverty rate was 15%. That's slightly less than the return on investment (ROI) that the 1% of the nation's richest people make on their investment. So you can clearly see that 15% is not a big number.

There are a whopping 314 million people living in the United States, or at least that's how many the Census Bureau was able to locate. It should be noted that finding 314 million of anything is a pretty darned big deal. Hats off to the Census Bureau for its effort. That's a lot of finding. Of the 314 million of us in this country, a paltry 46.5 million are considered poor. Yes, I can hear you blathering away that this doesn't depict the entire picture. This is just the wicked, down-and-out, very freakin' poor.

I know that only having a mere 46.5 million people living somewhat lower than dirt doesn't seem like all that much. It's certainly hasn't been enough for the top 1% to notice that's for sure. But leave it to CBS News to spoil the party. In July of 2013, they had the audacity to come out with a report that 80% of adults living in the United States are facing near-poverty and are unemployed.

OK, so the ladders of opportunity mentioned by President Obama above have a couple of rungs missing. In your case, it turned out to be one of the rungs at the top, thus causing you to crash right along with the rest of the economy. We can agree that it is now a cruel twist of fate that just when you're about to pull yourself up by your bootstraps (a position advocated by Rep. Paul Ryan, Sen. Rand Paul and Sen. Ted Cruz; all coincidentally pretty wealthy guys and nowhere near the poverty level), the bottom rungs of the ladders are now also missing.

Perhaps there is a rope or a step stool available that might give you a little boost so that you can reach that one rung way up there over your head. Shall we say a helping hand? Well, there was such a thing as unemployment benefits, which tragically expired right around Christmas of 2013. You'll be happy to know that the 1% did discuss this at their glittery Holiday Parties and did acknowledge that perhaps the timing was somewhat unfortunate, but justifiably appeared to lose interest in doing anything about it. After all, there was a platter of Petrossian caviar that needed their undivided attention. The last thing in the world these poor people could afford to have happen to them would be to lose out on that last bit of caviar while contemplating something that bares no relevance to them anyway. I mean, what do you expect these people to do about your poverty situation? They certainly are in no position to help you. They have troubles of their own; just like you used to have when you were one of them.

The time has come for you to cease feeling sorry for yourself, or worse yet, envious of others just because they were able to find a way to steal your money, job, home, etc., and begin the journey of climbing back up that wall of Recovery. Let's see if we can find a couple of extra rungs for that dilapidated, rung-less, ladder over there. You have work to do. Let's get busy.

CHAPTER 8

If You Can't Stand the Heat…

A while back I mentioned the Buchmayr Boys, a most interesting collection of triplets, who over time provided those who knew them with a near endless supply of remarkable adventures that would result in stories that would be passed down for generations. This in and of itself is somewhat odd as it was not like they solved world hunger or anything. Quite the contrary. If anything, it might be said that they created more problems than they solved but it was in the creation of the problem that lay the answer to so many questions. I can see that you're puzzled by all this.

OK, let me see if I can articulate more clearly for you in the form of a question. How hot must a small, well insulated room get before one's skin will begin to blister? Presumably this question has already raised a number of other questions in your head, which is good because it's already taking your mind off the doldrums in which you now find yourself. This one simple act alone should be enough to get you started down the road to Recovery, don't you think?

The Buchmayr Boys were always up for a good time. Come to think of it they WERE a good time. On their postage size lot sat an ancient house with a one-car garage off to the right. Out back was an old, unused shed. What's the point of having a shed if you're not going to use it? Two options were available regarding the shed. They could blow it up (they had a soft spot in their hearts for explosives) or they could renovate it and turn it into a 14 person Sauna. Inasmuch as dynamite was in short supply, it seemed like option #2 was the way to go.

There are Saunas and there are Saunas. I'm sure you've seen those pre-manufactured deals that set up in your closet and are operated with an electric heater that heats up the room with a handful of rocks. They work fine for one, maybe two people, and if you have one like this, I'm happy for you. It is not, however, what some of us would consider to be a Sauna. First, you need to ask yourself what's the reason to have a Sauna?

[87]

Well, you might think that it's to get really hot, clean out your pores from the inside out, and for all around good health.

In all likelihood, this is yet another example of your in-the-box thinking that is primarily responsible for you being in the shape you're in, which is not good shape. Sure, you hit on the obvious merits of a Sauna, but you left out the key reason; to get naked with awesome babes. Duh.

The transformation of the dilapidated shed into a world-class Sauna took place in about the same era as season #4 of Mad Men. If you've not seen Mad Men, stop reading right now and go watch every show of every season. Educating yourself on life in the '60s will give you a much better understanding of my friends, the Buchmayr Boys. They were those characters in this TV show. Sig worked on Wall Street and Charlie and Norbert were both ad men and were right up until the day they died. Sig left Wall Street and went into advertising as well. Picture Don Draper times three. Smart, dashing, dangerous, delightful scoundrels. They were much more upbeat than Draper, but it was this time of life when they lived. It was the three martini lunch era. Drinking and smoking were the norm. Partying hard was what they did. Were there times they had some trouble? Well, yeah, but it's hard to remember those times when your most vivid memory is watching someone's skin bubble up right before your very eyes. More on that unfortunate occurrence in a minute.

Building a Sauna requires imagination, basic knowledge of construction, and beer. Oh yeah, and some tools. We went to work gutting the old shed, which proved not to be too tough since there wasn't much in the way of interior walls to begin with. Norbert had the vision of how he wanted this Sauna to be. The rest of us were the string section in his orchestra. There was quite a crew working on this project. The Buchmayr Boys had an eclectic group of friends ranging from the well healed to locals, such as myself. They were as comfortable with the president of Field & Stream magazine as they were with a stone mason. They treated everyone the same. If you were honest, fun to be around, and could shoot straight (and knew enough to pull up should one of the brothers toss a clay pigeon at eye level), you could easily have ended up being friends for life with these guys.

Once the shed was gutted, some of us went about the task of insulating the walls (one nasty job on a good day), while Randy Auclaire and Roger Hayes went about the job of building the stove. If you have one of those wuss-ass electric Saunas, you skipped right over this part which is unfortunate because you missed a lot. Some people would simply put a woodstove in the room, build a chimney and call it a day. We weren't Some People. Slightly less engineering went into Sputnik than went into the creation of this Sauna stove.

After a long discussion that would inevitably lead into an argument, and nearly into a brawl thanks to plenty of beers, the concept behind the stove began to take shape. We didn't want to stoke the stove from inside the Sauna. There was the issue of smoke coming back into a room that would, before long, become so hot you could bake bread in there. Then, of course, there was the potential for dropping hot coals on the floor and burning the place to the ground. The best way to avoid both of these inconveniences was to stoke the stove from the outside. OK, but then how do you build the chimney so it's not going up inside the room?

Baffles. No, not as in we were baffled as to how to do this. From somewhere, there appeared a big piece of sheet steel about two feet long and about a foot wide. It was thick; real thick. If I was betting, I'd bet money that Roger Hayes, a.k.a. Foggy Hayes, was able to scrounge that up. Roger was not one to mess with. First off, he is a Hayes. If you know the family, I can stop right there, but since I'm hoping that this book makes it outside of Manchester, Vermont, it might be helpful to give you a little background on Roger.

He came from a typical Vermont farm family. His family's farm was the last farm in Downtown Manchester before it was sold to make way for more retail stores many years later. The family consisted of mom, dad, and four boys. Mom may have been outnumbered, but never out maneuvered. She might have been the toughest woman in the world. She had to be because she was surrounded by five of the toughest men Manchester ever produced. Had Vermont gone to war with anyone in the '60s, they would need only to have sent the Hayes boys to defend the state. The battle would last around 45 seconds. The enemy would take one look at these four brothers and quickly decide that it would be in their best interest to attack New Hampshire. Fight over. End of story.

At one time Roger had shaved his head with the exception of a long braid that he wore in the back. A Fu Manchu style moustache completed the look. It didn't hurt that he probably weighed around 230 (I'm being generous here in the event he reads this) and was as strong as anyone could be. The tiny farmhouse got a little cramped and the tension between four strong-willed brothers a little too intense so Roger moved out of the house. Now, that's not to say he moved away. He just moved out...onto the front porch. For years, people passing by the house that sat right on Rt. 7 (now Rt. 7A) would see a sleeping bag on a couch on the porch. Roger stayed out there year round for some time. FYI, it does get cold here in Vermont, but only for about 11 months or so. If you're sleeping out on your porch year round in Vermont, you are one tough cookie. Add to this the fact that with nothing more than a sideways glance, Roger could make most men die on the spot. He was strong, competent, and a damn good shot. He fit right in with this group.

Randy was working the cement. He began by building a very solid pad for his soon to be custom stove. The stove was made of block with fire bricks on the inside. Although built facing the outside for stoking purposes, the bulk of the stove protruded inside the large shed. About halfway up the stove, Randy laid some crossbars that would hold the river rocks. In addition to the bars for the rocks, he ran iron pipe in and around the upper chamber. Later the pipes would be connected to a 110 gallon wooden barrel that would hold water for splashing on the rocks as well as for washing up. It was really quite ingenious for the day. There was another steel plate that sat on top of the section of the stove that was in the room.

Wood siding was put up on the walls to cover the insulation and an amazing bench system was constructed. There were high and low benches. Obviously, the high benches were where you'd go if you wanted to take a very hot Sauna. If you couldn't take the heat, or wanted a break, you could jump down to the lower benches. A dozen or so wooden buckets like the ones Orvis used to sell were used for water with which to wash up.

Inasmuch as the Buchmayr Boys worked down country, this project was done on the weekends. I don't recall just how many weekends we worked on it, but it was a few. There came a time when it was completed. Man, was it slick. You entered a door that would bring you right in the middle of the room. To your left were high and low cedar benches that wrapped all the way around the room stopping on the wall to your right. The low bench stopped first; the high bench continued to the wall. The low bench had to stop to leave room for the monster barrel of water that would be heated thanks to the iron pipe built into the very clever stove. The room seemed to sparkle. Saunas are a winter sport. It's as much about the cold as it is the heat. When you spend some time in a 200+ degree room, you need to be able to chill out some. In lieu of waiting for winter, we had the good fortune of having a very tiny pond about forty feet away from the Sauna. It was more like a pool. It was about 15 feet in diameter and about 4 feet deep. The top was laid up of stone. It was charming and, if you were going to die, this would be a nice place to do so. More on that in a minute, too.

We did fire up the stove just to see if it would work as we had hoped. Randy was a genius and the stove worked better than anything you could have bought. It was amazing in its simplicity. We had no idea how long it would take to heat up 100 gallons of water and to bring the room up to temperature so we started the fire at around noon. We would take turns going outside and stoking and re-stoking the stove. Inside, high up on a shelf, we had an oven thermometer (similar to the one that I use today in my own Sauna) to give us an idea as to how hot the room was getting.

Inside the house, a party was raging. Everyone was working preparing dinner, which would consist of a slew of wild game. Earlier that morning, we had gone out partridge hunting; the most favorite thing in the world to do. We had about fifteen partridges and a few woodcocks. Add to this a ginormous bowl of pasta with Randy's special homemade pasta sauce, chased down with gallons of Chianti, and you were in for a terrific meal. There were plenty of attractive women running around; dates for the weekend. They tended to rotate week to week. It was tough to get real close to them as they probably weren't going to be around in a couple of weeks. That's just the way it was.

Around six o'clock, the Sauna was ready; actually it was more than ready. It was wicked freakin' hot. It was just under 300 degrees. Much debate ensued as to whether or not it was too hot to use. The debate quickly turned to an argument, but stopped shy of physical confrontation, thankfully. There was never any question that we were going to pile into this inferno of a room. We all ditched our clothes, grabbed a towel and marched out like lemmings on their way over the cliff. Diving off a cliff would have been cooler and less painful.

As soon as you walked into the room the heat seared your lungs. Your nose hairs dissolved instantly. You had to close your eyes for fear of them burning up right there in their sockets. Before the participants marched out to the Sauna someone went out there and filled all the buckets up with hot water and placed them on the floor slightly under the lower benches. Wash cloths were folded and placed neatly on the side of each bucket. They would come in handy.

Always the cautious one, I layed my towel down on the lower bench versus jumping right up to the upper bench. I sat on the bench to the left as you walked in. Roger sat right next to me. As local boys, we thought getting as far away from the stove as possible made the most sense. The city boys jumped right up on the high benches. We calculated their life expectancy at around 112 seconds. Norbert took what would become his perch in the upper right hand corner right near the 110 gallon wooden keg and the stove. He controlled the ladle that would eventually be used to sprinkle water on the rocks.

Oh, about the rocks. Prior to making the announcement that the Sauna was ready and we should all go out, Randy, Norbert and I went out to expose the rocks. Using insulated gloves, Randy removed the chunk of steel that made up the top of the stove inside the building. Doing so exposed the hottest rocks I've ever seen. The red glow of the rocks was nearly surreal. They appeared molten. They looked as though they were floating. They looked hot; really hot. Scary hot.

We all piled in. The first catastrophe came quickly. The women who had forgotten to move things like earrings and necklaces were the first to pay a pretty high price. The metal heated up within seconds. There was a fair amount of panic involved trying to remove various pieces. Some ladies were turned off immediately and went back inside. They wouldn't be back next weekend.

Once we got by the initial shock of a few ladies nearly catching fire, things settled down a bit. It didn't take long to realize that this room was way too hot. The only way to breathe was to dip your wash cloth into the wooden bucket of water between your feet and hold the wet washcloth over your mouth. It buffered the searing heat from destroying your lungs and it worked pretty well. There we sat; the survivors of the first wave of heat. We

[93]

were recovering from the initial blast, the screaming, the panic, the tears, and things were calming down a bit. We were adapting, or so we thought.

Sitting on his perch like the Cheshire Cat, Norbert, who had to be just sweltering up there, declared, "Maybe it's time we warmed this place up a bit." and with that he tossed a ladle of water on the rocks that resembled active nuclear fuel. Notice I didn't say he sprinkled the water on the rocks. No point in going halfway, I guess. The rocks hissed like a pail full of pissed off rattlesnakes. It was dark enough so that we couldn't see the massive cloud of instantly vaporized water that shot off the rocks.

One thousand one....one thousand two....one thousand threeEEEEEEEEEEE. So much for our plan about sitting as far away from the stove as possible to avoid the heat. Well, actually that plan did work for a while, but it failed miserably when the steam left the rocks, rose up and hit the ceiling, flew horizontally across the room at ceiling height, and then descended directly on top of Roger and me. It was at this moment that I witnessed a most amazing phenomenon. With the wet, white washcloth pressed firmly into my nose and mouth I looked to my right to see how Roger was doing. He was leaning forward giving me a good view of his very broad shoulders. In an instant, I could see tiny bubbles appear across his back.

"I wonder what those bubbles are about?" I thought to myself. One half of one nanosecond later, Roger was on his feet and out the door. I was right behind him. Really hot dry heat is one thing. Really hot wet heat is a whole other story. No one else got burned as badly as Roger did. He hung around outside for a bit and then decided to go back in. Most people would have been dressed and on their way home. Then again, they weren't sleeping on their porch at -10 degrees either. Maybe the thought of sleeping on the porch in January drove him back into a 250 degree room. Who knows?

Like anything else, we adapted to our surroundings and ended up having a rather enjoyable time. The dinner that followed was to die for. There was a great moment when Randy was lying on his back on the floor and someone was pouring Chianti into his mouth from about four feet up. No, it didn't all make it in his mouth. No one cared.

Fall turned into winter and we were taking Saunas now every Saturday night. It soon became a ritual. I was seventeen and had no idea at the time how incredible these times would be. It was hard to focus on the significance of the era when you're about to drown in a pond only four feet deep.

Later that winter, we were taking an exceptionally hot Sauna, maybe not as hot as the maiden voyage Sauna, but pretty damned hot. There came a time, as there always does, when we couldn't stand the heat one second longer. I blew out the door and ran full speed at the tiny pond. I dove in head first. I had it down. If I did a perfect dive dead center in the pond, when I came up, my hands would be right on the rocks on the opposite side. The outside temperature was around zero. It was really cold, but a quick dip in a pond after leaving a 220+ degree room was rather refreshing. The surface of the pond was devoid of ice because Siggy and I had spent a better part of the afternoon chopping up the ice with long handled axes. That's another fun job that I would have never done in a million years had it not been for the fact that I was doing it with Sig. I loved these guys a lot, mostly because we had crazy experiences that bonded us together unlike anything you might imagine.

I pulled myself up onto the slippery, now turning icy rocks and started to make a beeline back to the Sauna. My hair was starting to freeze (yes, I had hair then). As I was getting out of the pond, Roger had jumped in. Notice I didn't say dove in. Roger had not properly planned for his exit out of the pond. He was more focused on the instant gratification of getting cold. He started to pull himself out of the pond. The water that splashed up on the rocks froze instantly creating a too slick surface.

Roger slipped and fell back in the pond. Now, coming from a 220+ degree room and jumping into a frigid pond is rather refreshing. Falling back into that same pond is some fucking cold.

With eyes that spelled death to the one who would say no, Roger said, "Give me a hand" and extended his huge hand my way. I was slightly more focused on getting my freezing hair back into that 220+ degree room and had zero desire to turn around and pull a 230+ huge man out of a slippery rock-rimmed pond. Add to this the fact that I weighed 135 pounds and you can better understand my apprehension. There was a problem, though. Had I said no and gone back inside, which is exactly what my brain was demanding, and Roger had somehow lived, then I was automatically a dead man. I always say it's better to die with honor saving a friend than to have that friend tear your arms off and beat you to death with them.

I turned around and locked wrists with the extended hand. You would've thought that there might have been just a shred of gratitude in this gesture, wouldn't you? I'm sure there was but when a man as big as Roger Hayes is staring down the barrel of death's 12-gage, his brain is in survival mode. Hopefully, later, at my funeral, there would be plenty of time for gratitude.

I pulled as hard as I could. Roger got one knee up on the slippery rocks, then the other. Then he started to slip back into the pond. There was no way I was going to hold him. He gave a mighty yank and pulled himself out. Unfortunately, in doing so, the son-of-a-bitch yanked me head first back into the pond.

Let me pause a minute here to desperately try to find the words to help you to understand the meaning of the word COLD. I'm not talking about a little chilly-could-you-please-turn-up-the-thermostat-two-degrees kind of cold. I'm talking about COLD. So cold that your nuts will never again appear visible to the naked eye. Your penis will never, ever again be any larger than a raisin; EVER. Your heart doesn't just stop. It cracks into bloody red shards. Time stops kind of cold. Freeze frame. Done. Over and out.

I surfaced and the first thing I saw was Roger's hairy ass bolting back to the Sauna. Seriously, that bastard just left me there to die after I saved his sorry, albeit hairy ass. Revenge is a powerful emotion. That day it saved my life. There was no way that I was going to freeze to death and drown (or would I drown and then freeze to death. I never could come to grips with which one would've come first) before killing him.

Somehow I pulled myself out of the pond and flew back into the Sauna. I was about to punch Roger in the face, but before I could get the punch off, presumably because my arm was frozen and couldn't move, he said, "You got out." Nobody else in the room had any idea what he was talking about. I stood there for about 8 eternities thinking of the various ways I was going to kill Roger Hayes. I had no weapons available so I was simply going to have to use my hands to claw his eyes out, rip out his throat, reach down and grab his heart and pull that right out and stuff it up his hairy ass. It's always good to have a moment or two to ponder one's fate.

Looking at a somewhat confused Norbert Buchmayr I said, "Toss a little more water on those rocks, would ya?"

Roger Hayes and I have been friends ever since. Some things in life you really do recover from. If you're lucky you even get to laugh at them.

CHAPTER 9

Recovery Made Easy

It's a fact that recovery for some is much easier than it is for others. In your case, resting uncomfortably somewhere near whale shit on the ocean floor bottom, the Recovery may be slightly more difficult. For others, not so bad.

We learned today that 85 people share as much wealth as half of the entire world. Let's think about that. 85 people, about as many as might attend a large backyard barbeque, hold as much wealth as 3.5 BILLION PEOPLE.

Now, I know what you're thinking. What the hell is wrong with these people? How could they possibly have let 3.5 billion people have half of the wealth? There must be a way to grab that half and use it for the benefit of the 85 people who so desperately need it, right? I mean, life can get pretty darned scary when you have a billion or two dollars and then face the prospects of losing it all. Oh, right, uh sorry, that is what happened to you. Bummer.

Well, let's look at the bright side, then. You see, you can relate to both sides now. You should consider yourself one of the extremely lucky ones. Not everyone has been a member of that elite club; the 1% who pissed it all away only to land back down on the bottom. That takes some real hard work and brain power, for which you are to be commended.

So, where were we? 85 people control 50% of all of the world's wealth. Oddly enough, those who make up the 3.5 billion are probably too busy trying to figure out how they're going to make it until dinner time to be thinking all that much about this statistic. You can rest assured that those 85 are doing nothing else other than trying to find a way to shrink their number from 85, to 50, to 10, to 5, to 1. Think of it as an episode of that lame TV show, "Survivor" (yes, a rather appropriate name considering, don't you think?). Except in this show instead of having 10 or so people, we're starting off with 85. This is the first show of the season.

85 people stuck on a blue marble working to build coalitions of people who they know instinctively that they'll be screwing somewhere along the way. 85 people working hard to eliminate the person next to them, and the one next to him or her, so that the numbers decrease and someone gets closer to being the last person; the Survivor. What a great idea for TV show or maybe even a movie.

"The Hunger Games" had the same theme but with a lot more blood and violence than the TV show "Survivor". It should be pointed out that "The Hunger Games" was a book written for kids that was made into a movie. Let's get 'em while they're young. Survival is no laughing matter and if you're going to get to the top and be the last one standing, you're going to have to butcher a few people along the way. Kill or be killed. That's the message. If you don't want to play, no problem. You'll just fall down there with the other 3.5 billion people (soon to be all 7 billion people if the 85 have their way) and you'll be controlled like a farm animal.

Now don't get all down in the mouth about this. Some farm animals have a pretty good life here in Vermont. They're well cared for and have a nice barn in which to sleep. They're not that abused. Of course, there are the others who are beaten mercilessly and treated like shit. It would be wise to avoid ending up like one of these poor creatures. Farm animals that meet this criteria would be the black slaves that the 1% of a couple of hundred years ago thought would be a good idea to have around. You see, for the 1%, it's all about cheap labor, which is why the expensive move afoot to decimate labor unions. Having the chattel get together and piss and moan about working and living conditions does little more than cut profits. Without obnoxiously high profits, how do you expect one of the 85 people to end up being just one? It's small, selfish thinking like this that you exhibit that is holding back progress. Your job is to just go back out there in those fields and get to picking before the boss man lays that bullwhip across your back.

They don't want to hear you blatting about high unemployment or food stamps or clean water to drink. You have to stop worrying about things that are none of your business. The 85-soon-to-be-1 have plenty of good drinking water. They stole it from your neighbor after they eviscerated him. Yes, it's somewhat hurtful to lose all that you have, or worse have it stolen from you, but the sooner you understand the rules of the game that you're in, the better the chances you have of surviving. Your problem is that you are still living in the old-school world of right and wrong. You're trying to live your life honorably and do right by your neighbor and by your family. This is why, in all likelihood, you will never end up in that group of 85 people (it's not like they want you there anyway. Remember the game is to reduce that huge number down to something more manageable, like say, one).

It wasn't always this way on Planet Earth. Oh sure, there have always been the mega-rich. They had their holdings, did business amongst themselves, and didn't really bother anyone else. Although lord knows why they didn't appear compelled to have to own our government and buy those who run for office. There was some of that going on in the past, but today, it's now a matter of scale, or some might say a matter of survival.

For example, let's look at our friends and oil magnates, David and Charles Koch. OK, I can hear you now. Of those two descriptive words, "friends" and "oil magnates", you're taking issue with oil magnate. Good job and you're right. They do have other interests besides oil. They do appear to be somewhat interested in owning the country and you can't blame them. If they can't find a way to own and control our government, then it might be possible that our government would burden them with pesky regulations. Yes, there was a time, back in the good old days, when a company that was subjected to regulations so that the rest of us would have clean air to breath and clean water to drink would put up a fight, but in the end they would comply. By complying we would all be better off.

Not so much nowadays. Folks like the Koch brothers have finally been able to amass enough money that they might just be able to buy the state and local governments (since they're cheaper) and work their way right up to Washington. Right now, they can't do it on their own. Shamefully, they just don't have enough money and are forced to rely on a few of the equally wealthy friends to assist them in their quest.

There is something to be said for cheering them on and rooting for their success. This bloody battle for total control would make The Hunger Games look like a Mickey Mouse cartoon. It would be spectacular. Unfortunately, you would not have a TV being down as low as you are and, inasmuch as the Kochs would own all media, it's doubtful the slaying of the competition would be broadcast anyway. Then again, it could be a good-God-almighty show of strength to air the destruction of the competition. It would certainly give the rest of us pause should we get the hair brained idea to ever challenge them.

So now you're saying that this is not at all likely. Let's take a closer look at The Brothers. It was their father, Fred Koch, who invented the process of extracting gasoline from heavy crude oil. Damn good idea, too! It made him a ton of money. He had four sons whom he had hoped would be involved in the family business. They were. Once the old man died, the four boys sued each other for controlling interest in the corporation. The litigation went on for ten years; from the 1980s into the 1990s. The boys got their early hand-to-hand combat training by tearing each other to shreds. How perfect, really. These four delightful siblings were already writing the script for The Hunger Games and they didn't even know it.

Think of it. If you are willing to screw over your own brothers, screwing over total strangers should be pretty darned easy. Now, most of us haven't had the benefits of a life experience like the Koch brothers, which is why 3.5 billion share half the wealth and 85 people share the other half. You really shouldn't see anything wrong with this. It's nothing more than Darwin's

Theory of Evolution kicking in. Oh, you say that you're from the south and don't believe in evolution? OK, then think of it as creationism. The Koch brothers are God and they are creating your world for you. See that wasn't so hard.

----

85 people

BOB STANNARD, columnist
POSTED: 02/01/2014 01:00:00 AM EST

It's only 85 people. That's about as many people as might attend a small wedding, or a church service, or perhaps a controversial public meeting. Eighty-five people may live on your street, or just a fraction of your street. In the great scope of things, 85 people is not a lot of people. If you were asked to pull together a list of 85 people in all likelihood you could do it. Go ahead and try this exercise. Write up a list of 85 people that you know. Study this list very carefully. Now ask yourself this question -- what would you think if those people on your list of 85 people controlled half of the world's wealth; as much wealth as that of billions of people combined?

According to Oxfam, a British development charity that issued a report on the eve of the annual World Economic Forum meeting in Davos, Switzerland, 85 people control half of the world's wealth; i.e. $120.5 trillion. That is a lot of money. Look at the people on your list. Think about those 85 people controlling half of the world's wealth and ask yourself how good an idea is it that those 85 people, or any 85 people, have that much power and influence.

The World Economic Forum was created in 1971 by Klaus Schwab, a business professor at the University of Geneva. It was originally known as the European Management Forum, but apparently that title was deemed too restrictive. Sixteen years later the name was changed to the World Economic Forum. It was created, in part, to help resolve international conflicts.

Don't bother getting another part-time job so you can save up money to go to the next annual WEF meeting in Davos. From the beginning, it's been an invitation only event. In 1971, 444 business executives from Western European firms were invited to attend with a goal of learning more about American business management practices. Today, the WEF is funded by 1,000 corporations. Not just any corporations but global corporations doing roughly $5 billion per year. Joining these corporate executives at their annual meeting are public officials from around the world. This year, House Majority Leader, Rep. Eric Cantor, was in attendance. Other than leading the Tea Party element of Congress, it's a bit of a mystery as to why he would be invited, but, hey, I don't control the invitee list.

Only about 2,200 people from around the world get to participate in this five-day event that holds a variety of seminars consisting of international conflicts (a never ending problem), poverty (one wonders just what it is these mega-rich corporations have to say about this subject), and environmental problems (you might enjoy being a fly on the wall at this seminar as well).

So as not to run the risk of appearing secretive, the WEF invites hundreds of journalists from around the globe to attend any or all of the public sessions thus allowing the public to be kept fully informed as to what the world's wealthiest corporations are talking about, are worried about, and hopefully, what they are doing to address the perceived problems.

I've been to a couple of national legislative conferences, and yes, they were informative and there was much to learn at the numerous seminars I attended. However, I can assure you that I learned more about what was going on in other states over dinner and later at the bar talking with legislators from around the country. In Davos, we can only imagine who is meeting with whom after the public seminars and what issues of concern are discussed with the public eye blindfolded.

It may be a good thing that the wealthiest corporations of the world get together with political leaders to discuss how we might save the planet. I suppose if the planet is to be saved, these are folks who are in a position of influence to do it, don't you think? Of course, one might argue that it might be that it is some of the people attending this summit who are responsible for the problems for which they say they seek solutions.

Is it in the best interests of the 1,000 corporations to resolve world conflicts or is it in their best, financial interests to create world conflict? There never been any question that wars are good for business. Destroying the environment should not be a goal, but is there any doubt that in doing so a corporate bottom line might be increased?

All in all, it's a lot of fun for the couple of thousand participants. The really rich get to show off their wealth. The pols get to feel special hanging out with the mega-rich. The reporters get a week's worth of stories. Everybody wins.

Back to those 85 people. Suppose one of them was Gov. Chris Christie, a man who professes not to be a bully in spite of the fact that, as we're now learning, he is a bully. Is this the person you'd want controlling half of the world's wealth? Then again, maybe it is people like Christie who run the world.
    hen again, maybe it is people like Christie who run the world.

CHAPTER 10

Scratch if you Must

As you are beginning to learn (hopefully), there is survival and then there is survival.

"What's the difference?" you ask. It'd be best if you would remain silent so that we could just wonder if whether or not you're a moron, as opposed to opening your mouth and proving it.

There is the survival of the fittest, or as we would like to say, survival of two of the four Koch brothers. Then there's the survival of the rest of us. How do we survive from the moment we wake up until the moment we collapse and (try to) go to sleep? Granted your measly life is not nearly as complicated and dangerous as that of two brothers out to screw the world, but still you THINK it's pretty complicated and that's all that matters.

The following is a true story (or as true as I remember it to be). It's about the classic encounter between employee and employer. Pay attention here because this is about survival skills in wild, something that will undoubtedly come in handy somewhere down the line.

It was the fall of 1973, the year I was married and moved back to my hometown of Dorset. For those of you who were around then, you will recall that you could not buy a job. The oil recession had hit and gasoline was being rationed (remember the gas lines?). We were told that we were running out of oil which naturally led to a slight degree of panic amongst the masses. Of course, it was total bullshit. Turns out we have more oil than they led us to believe. Can you imagine the people in the oil business lying to the rest of us? Unheard of.

I was a long-hair back then and didn't much give a shit about anything. Life was carefree. Sure I needed a job and there were none to be had, but so what? I'd figure something out because I was a born survivalist.

[108]

I took a part-time job working for an old friend of our family, Dick Hayes. Yes, one of the Hayes brothers previously mentioned in this book. He was the oldest of four brothers and owned a construction company and a gravel pit. He was a very bright man with an engineering degree. He was also very persuasive. He had a big barrel chest, bald head, wore glasses, and when he spoke, you damned well had better listen for fear of getting your ass kicked. He had a fuse about 1/8" long and carried a lit match wherever he went. He was tough but fair; sort of.

He had me doing everything from extracting logs from a river that were placed there as a result of the flood of the summer of '73, to drilling and blasting out ledge to make way for new condominiums at a place that would be known as Bromley Village.

This particular day we weren't doing any of these things. It was pouring rain and the temperature was right around 43 degrees. I had toyed with the idea of just staying home, but thought better of it. Sure, I could've stayed home that one day…and then, most likely, every day after that. So, I went to work, which started at 7:00. Actually, it started at 6:00 am with breakfast at the VIP Diner. Most of Dick's crew started the day there with a coffee and muffin.

Dick came storming in (he never just entered a room; he stormed into it), looked around at everyone there who simultaneously looked straight down to the floor to avoid making eye contact with eyes that would set you on fire.

He looked at me and said, "You're coming with me."

That was that. No explanation. Nothing. Just a command. I paid my bill and left with Dick. We got in his remarkably dirty truck and off we went.

"Where we going?" I asked innocently.

"Don't worry about it." he replied, causing me to worry much more about it. We went up to this house in Manchester Village where Dick was doing the dirt work. The house was nearly complete. The driveway was in and all the outside needed was topsoil. Of course, we couldn't possibly be putting down topsoil today in the pouring rain. When you rake wet topsoil it balls up. Some of the balls of topsoil can get as big as a softball. Under no circumstances can you smooth out wet topsoil. My job today was to smooth out the wet topsoil in the pouring rain.

For outdoor gear I wore a pair of blue jeans (probably with long underwear), a couple of shirts, and a nylon, waist-length Air Force jacket. It was the closest thing I had to rain gear, notwithstanding the fact that it did not keep out so much as one drop of water. I knew that I would be soaked to the bone as soon as I stepped foot out of the truck.

Dick, on the other hand, had on a complete foul weather gear outfit. He had on the bright yellow pants with the elastic suspenders that crisscross over both shoulders. Covering his top half was the coordinated yellow slicker, complete with hood. Dick was not about to get wet. Naturally, Dick's job today would involve sitting in the enclosed, waterproof, heated cab of his lovely bulldozer.

I said, "Let me borrow your rain gear since I'm going to be outside and you're going to be in that dry, heated cab all morning".

He just stared at me and never said a word. It was like I had asked him for his entire bank account plus his new, shiny bulldozer to boot. His eyes made it pretty clear I was not getting his rain suit.

I stepped out of the truck, grabbed the metal rake, walked about 10 feet and I was soaked. Not unlike SCUBA diving, the layer of water between my skin and my chintzy nylon coat started to heat up. I wasn't all that comfortable but at least I felt as though I might not die within the next hour or so.

Dick was pushing the topsoil around with the bulldozer making a hell of a mess. I was desperately trying to rake it out so it's smooth to no avail. I was only able to reduce his giant balls of topsoil down to more manageable, smaller balls of topsoil. We were really getting nowhere but wet. Well, one of us anyway.

Suddenly Dick stopped the bulldozer. "He's finally come to his senses and realized that this is about the dumbest thing two people could be doing with their life." I thought to myself. No such luck.

One thing that everyone on Dick's crew knew about me was that I always carried a roll of toilet paper with me on the job. We were constantly being sent out to the middle of nowhere to cut trees for a new road that would be built behind the Chanticleer Restaurant or some other God-forsaken place. The last thing I was going to do was to wipe my butt with gravel because I didn't have any TP with me. As it turned out, wiping one's butt with gravel might not have been such a bad option.

Dick carefully put on his hood so as not to have one drop of rain come in contact with his skin. Gruffly he asked, "Do you have some toilet paper on you?" knowing full well I did.

"Yup"

"Give it to me." he demanded. "I gotta shit."

"It's twenty-five cents per square. How much do you want?" I replied.

"Fuck you. Give me the roll."

"Well, it looks like the price just went up to fifty-cents per square." I said not daring to take my eyes off his eyes.

"Stop fucking around. I gotta shit. Give me the goddamn roll!" he bellowed.

"We've just hit seventy-five cents per square. How many squares you want before we go to one dollar?" I asked sincerely fearing for my life.

"Listen you asshole, I'll go in that garage right there and rip some fiberglass insulation out of the wall and use that before I'll pay you anything for toilet paper." He was undoubtedly thinking that a wise choice earlier might have been to give me at least the rain coat.

"Have at it." I said and stood there defiantly with the steel rake firmly clutched in both hands.

"You're an asshole." he said and pushed the button to open the garage door. He walked right in and tore a big chunk of pink insulation out of the wall then proceeded out around back behind the building.

As I putted around moving a ball of topsoil from point A to point B, I couldn't help but wonder if Dick was able to take a shit without getting any part of him wet in the downpour rain. I wasn't curious enough to go see for myself. Eventually, Dick returned from his bonding with the out-of-doors. He stomped past me splattering my soaking wet jeans with mud that was once topsoil and climbed back up into the dozer like nothing had happened.

"Huh" I thought to myself. Now, if you know anything at all about pink fiberglass insulation, you know that you don't ever want to get any on your skin. Tiny shards of glass will work their way into your skin and make you itch like nobody's business. You can't wash it off. You can't really do much other than to let it just wear away. It doesn't bother some people. I hated pink insulation. I was starting to think that Dick might be one of those people who were unfazed by coming in contact with the Pink Panther, as it was known on construction jobs sites. Then, sure enough, he proved me wrong.

From my vantage point directly in front of the dozer, thinking that any minute he was going to bulldoze me right into the extremely wet and dysfunctional topsoil, I could see Dick slowly raise his right leg. The rain on the windshield distorted the human inside the cab but there was no mistaking seeing his right hand leave one of the levers used to maneuver the dozer and make its way back to his backside. He began to scratch.

The problem with having your butt-cheeks chock full of tiny glass fibers from wiping said butt with pink fiberglass insulation (aside from the obvious), is that once you scratch once you're fucked. It's like trying to eat one potato chip. You can't do it. Once you've caved into the burning, itching sensation and make the decision to go on the attack with that first scratch, then you are committed. It's best to really think it through, because after that first scratch there's no turning back. You'll be damned lucky if you have any butt left at all when you're done.

You'll get home and your poor wife will take one look at you and ask, "What the hell happened to you? Did you get attacked by a catamount?" (Just for the record, the Vermont Department of Fish and Wildlife adamantly denies that catamounts exist in Vermont, notwithstanding that a Vermonter shot one in the early 1900's. Therefore, it would be considered unwise to attempt to use the catamount as an excuse as to why your ass is torn to shreds.)

You know it's funny how things that were troubling only minutes ago seem to not be such a big deal moments later. Here I was soaking wet and freezing cold just minutes ago and now I wasn't even thinking about my miserable condition. Instead, I was having a good ol' laugh on the inside (one would never risk showing any external emotions at a time like this) watching my boss sitting up there in his dry, heated cabin of his lovely bulldozer tearing his ass right to pieces like nobody's business.

These are small victories that the 3.5 billion of us have come to relish. Sure we're never going to win; we're never going to be one of the 85 people who control half of the world's wealth, but maybe, just once in a while, we might be treated to the spectacle of watching them scratch an uncontrollable itch.

You can imagine this didn't last very long. Between the pouring rain, the uncooperative topsoil, and the extremely itchy ass, Dick finally came to the conclusion that this was not working. You can be assured that the ride back to the shop was incredibly quiet. He never said a word. Naturally, I was not about to say anything for fear of having to use a few squares of my toilet paper unnecessarily. Vermonters are a frugal lot and know enough not to piss away valuable resources just to get an unneeded dig in. No siree there was nothing to be gained by saying something like, "How's your ass doing?" or "Hey, can we stop in the store so I can get a SCRATCH-off ticket?" Nope, nothing to be gained there.

You don't gloat when you've taken one more step closer to survival. You just enjoy the moment and move on.

CHAPTER 11

Good Night Irene

Contending with the pitfalls of getting through a Recovery unscathed is not for the faint of heart. Great fortitude and inner strength is required if one is to survive a Recovery that proves to be much more exhausting than the original problem from which one is recovering. The case in point is that we have spent the last five years recovering from a Recession that lasted about five minutes. We didn't know what hit us and thus we had no real idea or plan as to how to get out of the mess we found ourselves.

You, who lost everything you own, have been bouncing around aimlessly like a BB in a 55-gallon drum. You're acting like the guy who finds himself in a round room and is told to go piss in the corner. It's bad enough that you're frustrated, scared, and bewildered, but add being clueless and you have a recipe for disaster. Fortunately for you I have taken it upon myself to write this book and offer some assistance to your otherwise hopeless situation.

What's the first thing you do when you lose everything? OK, the first thing you might do would be to go grab a bottle of Ripple Wine, crawl into a deserted car at the junkyard, get shitfaced, and remain there for a day or two until you can no longer stand the odor of your own body fluids. So, let's start with the second thing you would do.

The second first thing you should do is to find a way out of the situation you're in. Yes, I can hear you crying now, "Jesus, Bob, that's a shitload easier said than done."

No kidding, numbnuts. If this crap was easy, the Recovery would have been over in a wink. And by the way, things are always easier said than done. That's just the nature of things, so get over it. Finding one's way out of a precarious situation is, in a word, precarious. You find yourself questioning each and every move you make.

"Should I turn left? Should I turn right? Should I just stay right where I am? Oh, lord I don't know what to do. I'm paralyzed by fear." you rightfully say. The only difference between those who survive things like recessions, or any other calamity, and you is balls. It takes balls to make a decision when the burner is on high. Some try to figure out how to turn the runaway burner down. They're the first to go. Others try to put some distance between themselves and the white-hot flame.

There might be a better way to help explain this to you. Let's go back to August 28, 2011. That was a day that it rained some. The day before, the rained held off a bit. I had been invited to perform at the North River Blues Festival in Marshfield, Massachusetts. The producer of this, and other great festivals, John Hall, had not only asked me to play at the festival but insisted I stay with him and his partner, Ellie Johnson, at their place. This was a pretty high honor for a redneck harmonica player from Vermont, but John seems to like me. I've been invited to his shows for some time. He puts on an amazing two-day festival in August at the Marshfield Fairgrounds. He's a Blues fan and has had every great Blues player out there play at his festivals. For his day job, he works for Fed Ex. He doesn't play any instrument. He's just a Blues lover. If you're not a Blues fan, we understand how you might not get the obsession with this music. We sympathize for you.

The weather wasn't looking good. As a matter of fact, the forecast was for a hurricane to hit the east coast and work its way north to Vermont. Vermonters knew this was ridiculous because we don't have things like hurricanes and tornados. We have mountains that knock the snot out of the big storms while we sit back with a cold one and scoff. That might have been our first mistake.

The weather held off until almost the end of the show on August 27th. My first thought was that it might not be a half-bad idea to head back to Vermont right now even though this would mean driving in the rain in the dark. Been there; done that. Tossing logic off to the side, we went back to Ellie's condo and reminisced over the great music that we had heard all day long.

John Hall does more for the world of Blues music than any of the great players that he has play at his festivals. The players get paid. John takes all the risks. Why would a seemingly normal, intelligent man bother doing such a thing? He likes the music. Well, he likes the music and has more drive than 100 other people.

This barrel chested Boston "Southey" with blonde wavy hair is no pushover. There are two John Halls. There's the man who is kind, gentle, accommodating, a perfect host, and a pretty funny guy. Then there's the John Hall who, with nothing more than a sideways glance, can make your knees buckle. This man is all business. Hell, he has to be to have the longest, continuously operating Blues Festival in the Northeast. That's quite an accomplishment. You can check out his festivals at this website: http://rhythmroomrecords.com. We all like music. John has taken his passion for music to another level. There is nothing that makes him happier than seeing hundreds of people come together to hear the likes of Charlie Musselwhite, Mark Hummel, Rick Estrin, Mississippi Heat, Magic Slim and many other great players too numerous to mention here. Blues players and Blues fans from all around the Boston area are grateful for the good work this man does to preserve the genre.

Before retiring to bed on the night of August 27, John, Ellie, and I were staring at the weather station on the TV. The prognosis was not encouraging. A severe summer storm was engulfing Boston. Yup, I should've left hours ago. Could'a, would'a, should'a.

I awoke on the morning of August 28 to the sound of a freight train blasting through my room. I bolted upright and pulled back the blinds. What trees I could see were pressed over almost to a right angle. The rain was coming down horizontally. I had to get on the road.

John and Ellie were both up and coffee was on. "You want some pancakes?" Ellie asked.

"I don't know. I really think I should get on the road. It looks pretty bad out there."

"You can't leave without having Ellie's breakfast. Ellie makes the best breakfast in all of South Boston." said John in his heavy Boston accent. It was clear that "no thanks" was not an option so I said, "Sure, what the hell. How bad can it be out there? I've driven in rain before."

We were lounging around watching the weather channel along with watching the weather outside the window of the condo. It was really coming down hard and the wind was screaming. We didn't have a care in the world as the sausages were not quite ready.

For you poor souls out there who have not had the pleasure and privilege of having an Ellie Johnson breakfast, let it suffice to say that there's not a world-class diner/restaurant this side of the Mississippi that can hold a candle to her morning feast.

By the time I was done eating, I was ready to go back to bed for a nap. By now it was 10:00 am and the storm was raging. It seemed like about as good a time as any to hit the road.

"You drive carefully and give me a call when you get back to Vahmont." said John continuously expressing concern and care for my wellbeing. Hell, most of my friends could give a rat's ass if I made it back. John's a special guy.

We said our goodbyes and I got in my Honda Accord with only two payments left on the lease. The first thing I did was crank James Cotton's "Superharp" up on my Bose radio/CD system, light up a cigar, and hit the road. The music's loud. The hand rolled Dominican cigar is delicious. The wipers are on superfast trying to fend off the non-stop rain. I didn't have a care in the world. Bliss is generally the last emotion we feel just prior to the shit hitting the fan.

[119]

It was Sunday morning and I was going about 70 mph on Rt. 128. There's only one other car on the road and this guy was about 200 yards in front of me. My first thought was, "What a bunch of chickens. Why is nobody going out for a Sunday drive in this great stor....?"

I had not quite completed that thought when Mr. Boston in front was suddenly going sideways with a Tsunami wave of water coming over the top of his car via the passenger side. I was going downhill under an overpass. About a foot of water had gathered at the low point. Fortunately, thanks to Mr. Boston, when I hit the water it was down to only about 6 inches. I was able to reduce my speed down to about 45-50 mph when I hit the water. I know what you're thinking. Water has some give to it. This is true unless you hit a river going across Rt. 128 at 50mph. It's not quite like hitting a stone wall (yes, that task has been accomplished some time ago), but it's close.

After plowing through this mini-river, I decided that it might be in my best interest to take this adventure slightly more seriously. I backed off the gas, but not the music. I learned a long time ago that when you find yourself in really big trouble, it's not a bad idea to have James Cotton wailing away. The next two hours were reasonably uneventful.

I made it through Brattleboro, Vermont (or Vahmont as John would call it) without incident. I parked my car on the side of Rt. 30, because I just had to get out and look at the river that flows towards Brattleboro. On any given day, this river is about 100 feet below the road and is moderately shallow. This was no ordinary day. Three local teenagers were standing there with me. Eight eyeballs were transfixed on what was once a calm shallow river but now had morphed into a chocolate brown serpent swaying to and fro. It was about eight feet below the road instead of the normal 100 or so feet. This was not good. We could see full rolls of pink insulation and 16' 2x12's floating downstream.

"Which way you going?" one of the kids asked me.

"I'm heading to Manchester."

"Careful going through Newfane. I heaah the water's ovah the road up theah." said the kid with a great Vermont accent. It was time to move on. I came into Newfane and saw a river going across the road carrying with it building material from the local lumber yard. That explained the boards and insulation that I has witnessed back in Brattleboro. There was a car coming towards me. I decided to let him go first to see how deep this river was.

The car was going about 2mph. The water was just up to his door. He made it through. I was golden. I thought, "Well OK, we got this" and off I went zooming down Rt. 30 towards Manchester. Things were going along just fine. It had taken me two hours to get to Jamaica, Vermont. I was only 20 miles from home. I'd be there in no time…or so I thought. I had no way of knowing that the next two and a half hours of my life would consist of the most terrifying driving imaginable.

I drove through the tiny town of Jamaica and as I approached the bridge on the west end of town, there in the middle of the road stood a little old, Vermont man. He hadn't shaved in about two weeks. I had no reason to believe that he was going for new hipster unshaven look. I thought this was probably the way he was; just didn't get around to shaving.

He was wearing a yellow slicker with the hood pulled up over his black and red wool baseball hunting hat. He reminded me of just about every old Vermonter I had ever known. He puts both hands out in front of him like he was going to push me and my car backwards. It seemed like stopping was the right thing to do.

"What's up" I asked.

"Can't get through heeah. The bridge is out." the old Vermonter replied.

"How do I get to Manchester?" I asked

"Dunno."

"Why are you in charge of traffic?"

"Good question."

As you can see, this is a rather wordy conversation to be having with a Vermonter. The older ones aren't oftentimes this verbose. I got lucky. I backed up and took a high road that I had hoped would get me somewhere near getting back onto Rt. 30. My TomTom GPS device was losing its mind but after a bit recalculated my route. Rt. 30 was about a mile and a half dead ahead. Perfect. Crisis averted and soon I'd be back on schedule.

I came around a corner at 1.1 miles from Rt. 30 to find trouble staring me down. Red lights of the local fire truck were flashing away. It was not hard to see the tree that had snapped right off at about ten feet up from ground that was resting comfortably on the high tension wires causing them to sag low to the ground. They weren't so low that you couldn't drive underneath them, but the firemen were having none of it.

"Can I go through?" I asked.

"No, we're not letting anyone through." replied the fireman.

"They don't look like they can go much lower. I could just scoot right underneath them and be on my way." I said.

"You're not going under those wires." said the now stern and highly unfunny fireman

"In the length of time we've been talking about these wires, I could've been underneath them and on my way." I argued. Arguing is a big part of day to day life in Vermont. We argue

[122]

about everything. The weather. Politics. The roads. You name it and somewhere, at some local general store, there is an argument going on about something. Unfortunately for me, Mr. Fireman was in no mood to argue.

"You're not going under these Goddamn wires. Now turn around!" he said rather emphatically.

"How do I get to Manchester from here?" I queried.

"I don't know"

"Why are you in charge of traffic?"

"Get the hell out of here!"

That went about as well as could be expected under the circumstances. Were it not for this little setback I'd be minutes from my house. As it was now, I had no clue what to do next. TomTom was more useless than Mr. Fireman. I did what every Vermonter does when confronted with a no way out situation; I looked for a way out. I found a road that sort of felt like it might go in the right direction and took it.

I drove for what seemed like forever. I went by the now defunct Timber Ridge Ski Area coincidentally owned by my neighbor and good friend, Tim Waker. Tim bought the place years ago and no one could figure out why. In recent years, he's hosted rager parties for the snowboard community. It's a hell of a place for a party. Out of the way. No one gets hurt. Perfect.

The road I was on took me into Londonderry, Vermont. It was a little out of my way but not too bad, and again, I thought I should be home in about 25 minutes or so. I came around the corner and saw the familiar pond/river chocked full of lily pads, except I didn't see the familiar lily pads. The reason was that this usually mild mannered river had turned ugly on us and water was now about three feet over the road. Unbeknownst to

[123]

me at that time, on the other side of the flooded road, the local stores were four feet underwater. Londonderry was taking a beating.

I stopped the car and pondered my fate. Now what the hell do I do? In what can only be considered a most bizarre coincidence, parked right next to me was a midnight blue pickup truck with Mountain Plumbing & Heating inscribed on the door. The door opened up and sure enough there was my neighbor and owner of the defunct Timber Ridge Ski Area, Tim Waker.

"Yo, Tim. What's up? What are you doing here?"

"I was clearing brush over at Timber Ridge. Rain took on an edge. Thought it was time to head home." he said. "Looks like I hung on too long."

"Any idea which way we might go to get back to Manchester?" Tim asked the guy who was stopping traffic and keeping people from never being found again.

"Well, you might try going down that street back there on your right." he said. Inasmuch as this appeared to be our only option, we took his suggestion. In the meantime, we had picked up a family of four in an SUV from Albany, New York. The dad looked like he was having a pretty good time. The mom looked as though she could puke at any moment.

Always trying to be the guy to console those in need, I said to her, "Don't worry, things will be fine. We haven't lost anyone here in weeks." I could tell it helped.

We backed up and turned right off Rt. 11. We didn't get far before we noticed water going over this road, too.

Tim said, "I think I can probably make it in my truck, and Albany can probably do it in his rig, but I think you're fucked."

[124]

I squinted down the road and noticed these black dots going in a line off into the distance. I followed the line back to where we were standing and realized that the dots were the tops of the guardrails.

I said, "Tim, stand next to that guardrail" which he did. It came up to about his belt. Then I said, "See those dots out there in the water? I think those are the tops of the guardrails." It took a second for our new reality to sink in, but it was pretty clear that the water was about three feet over this road, too.

"Shit." said Tim. OK, let's turn around and take the back road to Landgrove through Weston and see what happens. We meandered our way through the back roads of Vermont and found ourselves coming into Weston. I should note here that we are going in the opposite direction from my house and we had been at this for well over an hour; closer to two hours. Pulling into downtown Weston did little to buoy our spirits.

Tim was in the lead followed closely by Albany and then me. We wanted to turn left at the historic and once beautiful village green, but there was too much water flowing down that street on the left. Tim sized up the situation as we drove into town and went straight before turning left in front of the also historic Weston Playhouse. We drove around the Town Green and parked in the middle of the road. Water coming from the brook up above us was flowing with an attitude. It had ripped out the septic system of the house on the corner. The smell of raw sewage in the air briefly allowed us to take our mind off the unfortunate situation in which we now found ourselves. I looked up the road to my right and saw something you don't see every day. The chocolate brown water was smashing into the side of the bridge that went over the river. The water would hit the bridge and fly about five feet in the air. The bridge served to push the water back. The river would regroup and attack the bridge again, and again, and again. It was apparent that the bridge could not withstand that kind of pounding forever.

Tim got out of his truck and immediately started walking right into the water. He got to the deepest part before turning around.

"OK, my boots are ten inches high. The water came just to the top of my boots so now we know how deep this is. There's only one way we're going to get you (meaning me) through this without your car stalling out. I'm going to back up and blast through this water. Albany, you do the same and stay right on my bumper, but DO NOT hit my truck."

Albany was grinning like the Cheshire Cat. His poor, pale wife looked terrible. His kids looked like they were having the time of their lives.

"Bob, you stay right on Albany's ass. If we do this right, we should be able to push the water back enough to get your car through." Tim said.

It was rather like Moses parting the seas. I was digging this. We all backed up and with no notice at all, Tim punched it and tore into the water. Albany had all he could do to get in line right behind Tim. Knowing Tim, I was not expecting much of a notice so I was ready. Albany plowed through and I hung tight to Albany's bumper. This worked slicker than hen shit. I drove through about two inches of water. I could see the water coming back together in my side mirror; not that I was spending a whole lot of time gawking in my side mirror. I was too busy white-knuckle driving through the water with one eye on the bumper in front of me and the other eye on the bridge up above me that I thought I could hear groan with every blow it took from the larger river.

Our little caravan headed up the hill and skirted over the near-failing bridge. We were off on our way to Landgrove. If we could get to Landgrove we could get to Rt. 30 and then home. Piece of cake. We've got this.

I was familiar with the road from Weston to Landgrove. Unfortunately, Tim decided to make a quick left turn down a road I had never been on. He had the pedal to the metal and was flying away from us. I had told Albany back in Weston that whatever happens, don't lose Tim. He knows where he's going. You don't. You'll be lost back here for decades. Albany's wife was desperately looking for a barf bag.

Initially, Albany slowed down a bit before fear started setting in. He stepped on the gas and off he went to catch up with Tim. I followed suit, but not for long. We got about 100 yards down this new dirt road when suddenly the road appeared to turn black just this side of Albany's back tires. There was a moment of confusion; then surprise was quickly followed by sheer panic. The road had collapsed just as Albany had driven over it. He never even knew what had happened. I, on the other hand, was confronted with a new reality. I was about to bury a Honda Accord, with only two payments left, directly head on into a ditch that appeared from nowhere. I stood on the brakes. The ABS system chattered away applying pressure as needed to the various four wheels. There was no way I was going to stop in time. I refused to close my eyes. I had to see this through.

The last thing I saw was the new, black ditch disappear under the hood of the Honda. "Oh boy, here we go." I thought, or was it screamed, to myself. The car came to a quick halt. I sat there motionless for a few seconds to make sure I was still alive. I put the car in reverse and very slowly backed up about ten feet before getting out of the car. I grabbed my camera and walked around the front of the car.

The road had, indeed, collapsed entirely across both lanes. It was about eight feet across and about six feet deep. It would have a made a perfect final resting place. Thankfully, it wasn't my time. I backed up, turned around, and went back to the Landgrove Road. I was still shaking when I encountered a family walking down the road. I thought it wise to stop and ask for directions.

"Any idea how to get to Rt. 30?"

"Well, you can go up and over that mountain road right there on your right but it might be washed out a little ways up the road." the mom said. Not helpful.

"What if I go straight?"

"Yes, that will also take you to there, but I don't know what condition that road is in."

OK, so the options were to take the mountain road that we were pretty sure was washed out, or take the Landgrove Road that might not be washed out. Not much to think about here. I thanked the family and told them to be careful and headed off towards Rt. 30.

Two hours and fifteen minutes after I had encountered the fallen trees lying on the wires and the somewhat grumpy fireman, lo and behold, right before my eyes, is yet another fallen tree lying on the power lines. This time, the lines are a little lower, but it did look like I could fit underneath them. Sure enough, there were two local firemen there whose job it was to keep people from going past these downed lines. TomTom said I was one-tenth of a mile from Rt. 30. ONE FUCKING TENTH OF A MILE. I'd been turned around about half dozen times and I was running out of routes to take. If I turned around now, I would have to go back through Weston (without the aid of the water-parters) and make my way north up to Rutland. Little did I know that Rt. 7 was completely taken out across both lanes in Clarendon. Had I gone north, I would have been stranded.

Fireman A was leaning on the door talking to Fireman B through the open window. They were distracted. I was focused. I stepped on the gas and blew around the firemen who were yelling profusely saying, "Hey, can't go through there!!!" Too little, too late.

Within seconds, I was on Rt. 30. I couldn't believe that I had made it. The rest of the trip home, only about ten miles, was uneventful. Throughout the ordeal, I was calling my wife, Alison, who was home with our visiting daughter, Meredith. They were telling me how bad the weather was and how insane I was to be driving in this storm and how could I have possibly gone all the way down to Boston knowing this storm was coming, just to play music. I knew that the fear of having our house blow away was clouding her judgment. She knows the power of the Blues.

I got home and immediately called Tim to see how he made out. His wife, Sue, answered the phone and said he wasn't home yet. Uh oh. This wasn't good. I found out a couple of days later that the road up ahead of where Tim went was underwater. He and Albany turned back around only to discover that the road had collapsed. They saw the skid marks. When I told Tim that those were my skid marks he said, "Bet you just about shit your pants." It was close.

So what did Tim do? How did he ever get home? Adversity is the mother of invention, or something like that. Turned out he knew a guy who lived near the river who happened to have a backhoe. Tim asked if he could use it for a minute to fill the road in. "Sure." the Vermonter said. Tim filled in the road by himself and was able to drive out of the predicament he had found himself in.

He got home about an hour or so after I did. We never did hear anything about Albany but we didn't read anything horrible in the papers so we assumed he, too made it home safe and sound. All in all, it was a most exciting ride home and real learning experience. You should consider yourself lucky that I decided to share this with you. This could save your life. You might consider taking a lesson or two in how to operate a backhoe if you have the time.

CHAPTER 12

You Call This A Recovery?

It's easy to understand why you might not understand why it is that Vermonters, for the most part, see solutions to things like Recessions and Recovery more clearly than the average person. Perhaps the answer lies in the fact that the people who moved to this one-time Indian hunting ground were pretty independently minded folks.

The article below, written almost a decade and a half ago, might help you to better understand the crazy people who lived here and raised families here, some of which have tried their damnedest to remain here in spite of overwhelming odds. It's not an easy place to live. It seems like we have around eleven months of winter augmented by 30 days of bad weather.

To make a living here, you either have to have made your fortune elsewhere and moved here (which doesn't qualify as making a living here) or have two, three or four jobs to make ends meet. Our taxes are high compared to other states. Those who can afford to do so, live here six months (the ones that are the least like winter) and then head down to Florida for the other six for fear of actually coming in contact with snow. These folks are known as "snowbirds" as they are seen as flying south for the winter.

Those who remain behind know that every day they wake up is most likely going to be a day filled with adversity and struggle. Wages are lower here than anywhere else. It's hard to earn a living farming as the huge farms in the Midwest eat our lunch, so to speak. However, in spite of all of the reasons to not live here, 600,000 or so crazy people do live here. They get hard times, because, for the most part, they've never known anything else. Few people born and raised here are getting rich, but damn near all of them are getting by. They've known for a long time that there are two kinds of rich. There is rich as in having a ton of money, and rich as in having a rich life. Vermonters would take the latter any day which is pretty much why they're poor money-wise. When talking to a Vermonter in your new Mercedes that has slid off the road because winter came early and you still have all-season tires on your car, and because you didn't get out of the State quickly enough, it would be unwise to say, "You don't look rich to me." Should you offer up this opinion, you can count on one of two things happening: A) you will never get out of the ditch you're in or B) you'll get pulled out and it will cost you a fortune resulting in you being less rich and that guy who pulled you out, just had his wealth go up significantly.

Here's the piece about my ancestors:

Migration: A Story of Vermont Before 1850

Scott Andrew Bartley Published Date : May 5, 2000

A researcher cannot hope to truly understand Vermont history without first studying the migratory history of the region. Vermont's history is all about people on the move, in search of that better life beyond the congestion of the big cities and towns of southern New England. It is also about a political way of life. That, however, is a subject for another time. Let us turn our attention to the first settlements in Vermont.

The Abenaki Indians, and other tribes, were the original Vermonters. The French had been visiting the region since 1609 but had not established a permanent settlement. Massachusetts granted lands in southern Vermont in 1716 and built a fort in the "Great Meadows" called Fort Dummer (now in the town of Dummerston) in 1724. The French established themselves along the eastern shores of Lake Champlain in 1731. Vermont was still a frontier, with heavily forested lands, and far from the thriving ports on the coast or major rivers. Travel was difficult, usually done on Indian trails or the frozen pathways of the winter's rivers and brooks. The first major settlement commenced in 1749 around the Bennington area and the southernmost tier of towns nestled along the newly defined Massachusetts border with New Hampshire established by King George II in 1740.

New Hampshire seized this opportunity and granted many towns to groups of people called "proprietors" until 1754.

The constant raids and uncertainty of the French and Indian War from 1755 to 1763 almost completely stopped the flow of settlers. It was that war, however, that brought news of the new land so green and unsettled and provided the impetus to build several roads into the region. The first was the Crown Point Road, which was constructed from the Fort at No. 4 (Charlestown, N.H.) and Crown Point, N.Y., from 1759 to 1760. New Hampshire resumed its granting again until 1764. The politics of the time created a major dispute between that state and New York over legal claims to the land in present-day Vermont. The political winds of the time sided with New York, but the migration to Vermont was already in full swing. Not even the actions of New York invalidating the New Hampshire Grants stemmed the tide.

This migration was a multistage process. Families often lived for a short period of time in various communities along their way to Vermont. People poured into the Grants, as they were known, coming up the Connecticut River valley on the east. These settlers were generally from the east side of southern New England. People in southeastern Massachusetts would move through Rhode Island or eastern Connecticut. They would make their way west to the Connecticut River towns in northern Connecticut or western Massachusetts, called the "Pioneer Valley." This would be the launching point to their final destinations within eastern Vermont. Immigrants from the Boston area and just north and west usually moved into the heart of Worcester County or the northern fringe towns close to New Hampshire. From there, they went directly west, again to the Connecticut River, or briefly settled in the towns of southwestern New Hampshire before making their way to the central and northern parts of eastern Vermont.

Settlers also used the Hudson River to enter on the western side of the mountains. They often came from western regions of

Connecticut and Massachusetts; others came to Vermont from the several counties above New York City, where they had settled earlier. These settlers filled the counties of Bennington and Addison, as well as the northern reaches around Burlington. A smaller influx came from the "Upper Valley" region of New Hampshire, moving to the Northeast Kingdom (basically Essex County).

These migration patterns were the norm, but there were exceptions, as illustrated by the following examples. The Scots moved to Barnet and Ryegate in the early 1770s. The Irish were in Vermont as early as 1774, though settled in earnest between 1816 and 1822 from Quebec City. The Quakers first settled in Danby in 1780. They soon spread into Ferrisburg, Starksboro, South Hero and other places from Rhode Island, Massachusetts, and Nine Partners, N.Y. The families of Ellsworth, N.H., moved en masse to Sharon, save five families that remained behind. My own ancestry provides another fascinating story.

William4 Olney and his wife Alice Dexter were living in Smithfield, R.I.. They took their family, including their adult children, up to Sackville, New Brunswick, then to Nova Scotia, in 1761 when the British were trying to repopulate the Acadian region with hearty New England stock. William and Alice both died there. The children began to have children of their own before many of them returned to New England, most by 1774. Their son Abraham and his wife Esther Young were among them. Soon they joined the migration to Vermont. They likely stopped somewhere in between but ended up in Springfield, Vt., where many descendants now live. The records show that all of these children were born in Nova Scotia -- not a place most researchers would suspect!

The American Revolution was a turning point for migration. People moved about much more freely and the flow of settlers increased. Vermont, some thought, would become the most populated state. A case in point was Vergennes, established as a city in 1788. Another would not be designated for almost 100 years. The irony here is that the city is no bigger now than it was 200 years ago. The majority of Vermont towns, in fact, peaked in population between 1810 and 1830. French Canadians started moving south from Eastern Townships of Quebec, then called Canada East or Lower Canada. Their numbers swelled between 1808 and 1820. Many of them were Catholic, but it was not uncommon to see them convert to Methodism. The migration was sometimes disguised by name changes or corruptions such as LeBrun, which became Brown, Beausoleil to Son, and so on.

Great changes were on the horizon. The newly independent state of Vermont was formed in 1777. With it was the first great out-migration. Loyalists from all over the colonies started moving to Quebec and Ontario between 1776 and 1783. Vermont helped motivate this group by confiscating their land to support the state treasury and its war effort. Few of them ever returned.

After the war ended and peace across the borders was secured, the frontiers were now safe for general pioneering. Vermonters answered that call in numbers larger than those that came to Vermont a generation before them. People moved up the Connecticut River valley through St. Johnsbury and into the Eastern Townships. Greater numbers headed through the valleys west and out of the state. One diary often quoted made note that on a single winter's day in 1795, more than 500 sleighs filled with families moving west came through Albany, N.Y. The Northwest Territories was set up in 1787, drawing many there. The "Genesee Fever" and other named massive exoduses called Vermonters to central New York, Pennsylvania, and beyond. The first wave of Vermonters who settled upstate New York along the Canadian border became the dominant group. Lake Champlain and the Saint Lawrence River were the "roads" to the Great Lakes region and settlement in Michigan and Wisconsin.

Vermont history is truly one of migration. Its history shows it ballooning with people eager to start a new life beyond the regimented ways in old New England. As soon as the balloon was filled, it was deflated with its people pushing further into the new frontier. They came to Vermont for many reasons, and they left her for the very same ones!

[136]

The author opted to skip over the "political way of life" as he referred to Vermont's way of life. I can understand why. It's complicated. For about 200 years or so, Vermont was a staunch Republican state. Remember it was the Republican Party that supported the freeing of slaves and southern Democrats who fought that initiative tooth and claw. Funny how times change. Although Vermont was predominately a Republican state, it was a different kind of Republican Party than we see today. These old Vermont Republicans were very careful with a buck, predominantly because they didn't have very many. However, they were also very caring. Some of the most socially progressive laws that exist in this state were adopted by Republicans. It was Republicans who adopted strict land use development legislation and banned billboards in this state. Social safety nets established many years ago were Republican initiatives.

If all this is causing you to scratch your head a little, you might recall that our Republican United States Senator, Jim Jeffords, abandoned his party of generations. In doing so, he tipped the scales of the makeup of the U.S. Senate in favor of the Democrats. Then president, George W. Bush, had to have been some pissed and I expect he was. However, it should be noted that, for the most part, Sen. Jeffords was regarded as a hero in his home state. He demonstrated a level of independence that is the foundation of politics in Vermont.

Vermont is one of the few states where you don't register to vote by party. Anyone can vote in any party primary that they choose. It would be considered unwise, and possible detrimental to your health, if you were to advocate otherwise. Vermonters do have trouble being told what to do. This all comes from a long line of people who have made Vermont what it is; people who left the big cities and heavy religious pressure in hopes of being able to just live. They didn't give a shit if they were poor. They were happy to just survive and be left alone. If you think about this for half a second, you might agree that their philosophy on life was not a bad one. If more people minded their own business and stopped trying to push their religious agenda on the rest of us, the world might not be such a bad place.

The last topic in the world that you would ever want to talk about with a Vermonter is your religious beliefs. Should you ever feel compelled to do so, let me offer this advice; we don't give a rat's ass what religion you are or choose to practice. You are free to worship any way you so choose. However, should you run around and try to impose your religious beliefs on those who live here, either by passing out shit at the local store, or trying to do something legislatively, you can be assured that you will get your ass kicked. What you do is your business. What I do is mine. Let's not meld the two for fear of someone getting hurt and it won't be me.

So now that this is behind us and we know who we're dealing with, don't make the mistake of thinking that Vermonters don't give a shit about anything. They are probably the most opinionated species on the planet. They have an opinion on everything from national and world affairs to what's up with the new library and everything in between. We see a difference between expressing one's opinion and trying to force another to accept our point of view. Unless, of course, we go to war over something then all bets are off.

It was the Vermont Brigade, under the leadership of Gen. George Jerrison Stannard (yes, he's an ancestor, no less), that defeated Gen. Pickett at Pickett's Charge in Gettysburg. It's commonly believed that Pickett said, "If it wasn't for those fucking Vermonters, we would have won the war." He was probably right. Per capita, more people fought in the Civil War from Vermont than any other state.

Now you may be asking yourself why would people who moved to this state to get away from the conflict of big cities choose to go fight in a war to free slaves down on the other side of the country. The answer to that question is easy once you understand Vermonters. In all likelihood, they didn't much care for the idea of someone's independence and freedom being taken away, no matter what color they were. Vermonters, probably better than most, understood that if blacks could be subjected to a life of slavery than very possibly so might Vermonters. It was best to nip that shit right in the bud.

So here we are today trying to survive the booming Recovery that we're theoretically going through. In order to survive, it's important to understand just what it is that we're supposed to be surviving from. Once we have that figured out, the rest should just fall into place, don't you think? Let's take a look at how we got into the Recovery mess to begin with.

To recover from a Recession we first had to have a Recession. We all get that. We had a Recession primarily because we had a whole lot of bad loans made to home buyers. Those loans were cleverly bundled together and sold. Those cagey bankers knew what they were doing. Just to cover their collective asses, they insured the bundled loans. That, too, was a great move. Everything was going along famously until it wasn't. The shit hit the fan.

Walking into his new job, President Obama was confronted with a huge problem, but fortunately it came with a solution put forth by the previous administration who oversaw the collapse of the global economy. Pretty darned thoughtful, we thought up here. You help to create a problem, but then at least you step right up and offer to fix it.

Of course, we all know now that the fix was to give a trillion dollars to those who helped create the problem. The banks took our money and did the only thing that made sense, to them anyway, which was to hold onto it for a while. They're still pretty much holding on to it today. Not all of it, mind you. They had to give $28 million a year to Jamie Dimon to add to

[139]

his overall net worth of $400 million. That seems fair, right? It's a shame, really, that he's only worth $400 million. Imagine how inferior he must feel when he's at a party somewhere and runs into someone worth a billion. It must depress him terribly. And he suffers this way because you, you cheap bastard, wouldn't come up with some more money to give to the banks.

So we had a Recession. Presumably some of you won't agree with the above assessment on how we ended up with a Recession and that's OK. You should know, much like my ancestors, I couldn't give a shit what you think, so think away.

The Recovery is an entirely different story. Hell, anyone can survive a Recession, but surviving a Recovery is a real challenge and not for the faint of heart. First, you need to have a great deal more understand and sympathy for those who are extremely wealthy. If you can't find it within yourself to show pity for your fellow man, it's going to be very hard for you to recover. You see, the folks at the top of the food chain lost a ton of money. Some went from something like $800 million down to $500 million. A drop like that can be a real shock to the system and require some real adjustment to one's lifestyle. It's not easy losing that much money. Of course, it is slightly easier if you have a shit-ton of money to begin with.

Fortunately, the Recovery has helped to alleviate the misfortune bestowed on the wealthy because of the Recession. Now I can hear you wining that the Recovery has not done one goddamn thing to help you. It's uncanny how selfish you can be. You should stop thinking about yourself and focus more on others. You'll feel much better. Now, if you were a Vermonter, you would focus your efforts on those less fortunate. If you're an American banker, you would focus your efforts on, well, you.

The piece below, written by Les Leopold, might help to frame where we are and how we got here.

The Rich Have Gained $5.6 Trillion in the 'Recovery,' While the Rest of Us Have Lost $669 Billion *It's no accident.*

Photo Credit: Shutterstock.com/ durantelallera

May 3, 2013 |

Oh, are we getting ripped off. And now we've got the data to prove it. From 2009 to 2011, the richest 8 million families (the top 7%) on average saw their wealth rise from $1.7 million to $2.5 million each. Meanwhile the rest of us -- the bottom 93% (that's 111 million families) -- suffered on average a decline of $6,000 each.

Do the math and you'll discover that the top 7% gained a whopping $5.6 trillion in net worth (assets minus liabilities) while the rest of lost $669 billion. Their wealth went up by 28% while ours went down by 4 percent.

It's as if the entire economic recovery is going into the pockets of the rich. And that's no accident. Here's why.

1. The bailouts went to Wall Street, not to Main Street.

The federal government and Federal Reserve poured trillions of dollars into Wall Street through a wide variety of financial maneuvers, many of which were hidden from view until recently. When we add it all up, it's clear that most of the money floated right into Wall Street. (Fannie and Freddie were private institutions that also considered themselves part of the Wall Street elite.)

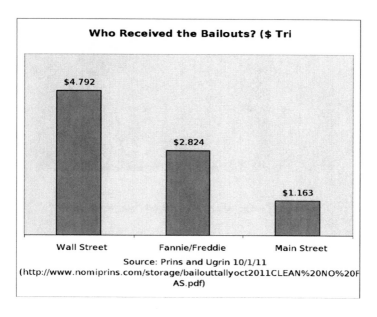

Who Received the Bailouts? ($ Tri

Source: Prins and Ugrin 10/1/11
(http://www.nomiprins.com/storage/bailouttallyoct2011CLEAN%20NO%20F
AS.pdf)

2. Wall Street is Washington, Washington is Wall Street.

Those who shuttle back and forth between Washington and Wall Street designed the basic policies that both led to the crash and that responded to it. Hank Paulson, Bush's Secretary of the Treasury, served as chairman of Goldman Sachs before going to Washington. Timothy Geithner, Obama's Secretary of the Treasury, headed the regional Federal Reserve Board in New York (a board composed of Wall Street's Who's Who) before joining the Obama cabinet. Countless government officials and congressional staffers can't wait to leave public service for lucrative jobs on Wall

Street. Their collective mindset is that the world can't function properly unless the richest of the rich get richer. Any and all policies should therefore protect our biggest banks, rather than hinder them. And, of course, both parties are in hot pursuit of Wall Street campaign cash. Little wonder the so-called "Recovery" transferred wealth from us to them.

3. The Federal Reserve banks on trickledown.

The Federal Reserve's ongoing stimulus policy comes down to this: The goal is to reduce interest rates on bonds of all kinds so that money flows into stocks. The more money that goes into the stock market, the higher go the stocks. Rising stock prices leads to what economists call the wealth effect -- those who see their stocks rise dramatically feel richer and spend more. That's supposed to trickle down to the rest of us: The rich spend more, businesses recover and then, maybe, hire more people. It's working beautifully for the super-rich but obviously not for the rest of us.

But wait, don't most of us own stocks either directly or through our pension funds and 401ks? Dream on, says this chart:

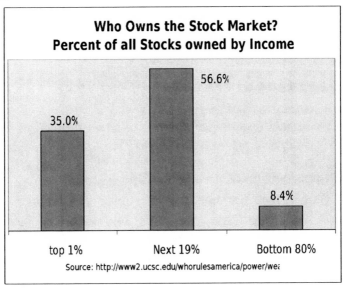

Who Owns the Stock Market?
Percent of all Stocks owned by Income

56.6%

35.0%

8.4%

top 1%   Next 19%   Bottom 80%

Source: http://www2.ucsc.edu/whorulesamerica/power/we

4. Washington fails to create enough jobs.

Wall Street's gambling spree tore a gaping hole in our economy. In a matter of months, more than 8 million workers lost their jobs due to no fault of their own. What these elite financiers did to us is unconscionable,and they haven't had to pay a dime for the damage they caused. Although the stimulus programs prevented the slide from deepening, it was far too small to put America back to work. So now we're facing the highest levels of sustained unemployment since the Great Depression. The biggest victims of Wall Street greed are the long-term unemployed.

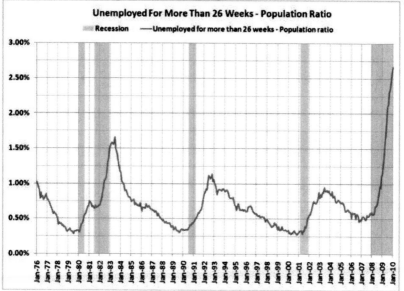

Source: Business Insider:
http://www.businessinsider.com/unemployed-for-more-than-26-weeks-population-ratio-january-2010-2

5. Government goes on a job-killing spree.

After Wall Street crashed the economy, businesses failed, workers lost their jobs, and state and local tax revenues collapsed. In a just world, Wall Street would have been taxed to make up the difference. Instead, public employment was slashed. This further cut back on consumer demand, reduced tax revenues, and then created pressure for another round of government job cuts. Of course, the Tea Party right loves the idea of crushing government jobs and public employee unions as well. But the main result is to increase unemployment, which in turn puts downward pressure on wages and increases profits for the wealthy.

As Michael Greenstone and Adam Looney point out ("A Record Decline in Government Jobs: Implications for the Economy and America's Workforce"), "We are in unchartered territory when it comes to government employment." The chart below from their Brookings article shows that among the major state and local job categories, only firefighters saw an increase.

Occupation	Employment (2009)	Employment (2011)	Change in Employment	Percent Change in Employment
Teachers	3,942,700	3,721,938	-220,762	-5.6%
Policemen	666,579	610,427	-56,125	-8.4%
Fire fighters	233,051	277,158	44,107	18.9%
Emergency responders	69,370	39,170	-30,200	-43.5%
Air-traffic controllers	23,959	17,128	-6,831	-28.5%

Overall, the combination of state, local, and foolish federal cutbacks is collapsing public employment like never before. And again, whenever unemployment increases, it places downward pressure on the wages and reduces the wealth of the many, while the few are enriched.

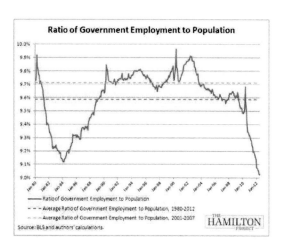

Ratio of Government Employment to Population

— Ratio of Government Employment to Population
- - - Average Ratio of Government Employment to Population, 1980-2012
- - - Average Ratio of Government Employment to Population, 2001-2007
Source: BLS and authors' calculations.

THE HAMILTON PROJECT

6. The big banks have become even bigger criminal conspiracies.

Not only did we bail out too-big-to fail banks with public money and got nothing back in return, but Washington allowed them to grow even bigger. The biggest banks now have oligopoly power to rig prices. They also can illegally collude in order to siphon off more wealth from the rest of us. (For some juicy details, see Matt Taibbi's "Everything is Rigged: The Biggest Price-Fixing Scandal Ever.") The corruption and cheating are reaching epic proportions as they gamble with insured deposit money, partner with loan sharks, money launder for drug cartels, and foreclose on homeowners who are up-to-date on their payments. All of that dirty money goes to the rich. (See "Are Big Banks Organized Criminal Conspiracies?")

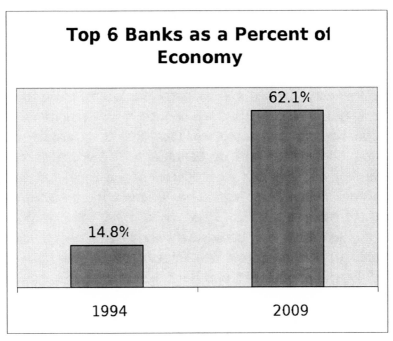

Top 6 Banks as a Percent of Economy

62.1%

14.8%

1994

2009

Source: Federal Reserve
http://www.ffiec.gov/nicpubweb/nicweb/Top50Form.aspx

7. Hedge funds run wild.

In 2012, the top hedge fund manager "earned" in one hour as much as the average family makes in 21 years. The top 10 hedge fund managers made as much in one year as 196,000 registered nurses. What exactly do these hedge fund honchos do? Much of it comes from what normal people call cheating -- some of it legal, some of it borderline, and much of it criminal. But they're hard to catch. They profit from illegal insider tips, high frequency trading, rumor-mongering, front-running trades, special tax loopholes, and even by creating financial products that are designed to fail so that they can collect the insurance. They have their hands in our pockets 24/7. (See "America's New Math: 1 Wall Street Hour = 21 Years of Hard Work For the Rest of Us.")

[147]

8. The rise of the Ayn Rand Right.

The Tea Party brought a new viciousness to the national dialogue. Not only do they hate the government, but also, they hate the poor. Using the twisted logic of Ayn Rand, they see the world divided into winners and losers -- and screw the losers. Not only do they oppose social programs like Social Security and Medicare, they also don't believe that government should work on behalf of the collective good. In fact, they see any and all collective efforts as an affront to personal liberty. They want a world where the creators rule and the moochers suffer. They would rather the rich rob us blind, than have the government try to stop the financial cheating and deception. If Wall Street destroys your job -- too bad. Go get another one and don't expect the government to help.

9. The silencing of Occupy Wall Street.

For a few short months, the hundreds of Occupy Wall Street encampments dramatically shifted the national debate. Wall Street was in the crosshairs and "We are the 99 percent" spread into our consciousness. It's still there, but Occupy Wall Street isn't...at least not in the potent form that shook the rich and powerful. We don't have time here to discuss whether it was silenced by repressive authorities, or if it primarily caved in due to internal weaknesses in strategy and tactics. But this much is certain, a mass movement to take on Wall Street makes a difference.

***

The solutions are simple, but the fight is hard.
The Robin Hood Tax

The best way to move money from Wall Street to Main Street is through a financial transaction tax -- a small charge on each and every sale of stocks, bonds, and derivatives of all kinds. Consider it a sin tax on Wall Street's many vices. Such a tax could raise enough money so that every student in this country could go to a two or four-year public college or university, tuition-free. Just think what the elimination of increasing student debt would do to the lopsided wealth statistics. Just think of what that would do for jobs as colleges expanded to deal with the demand. It's not a wild-eyed demand: 11 countries are about to adopt such a tax. (See robinhoodtax.org)

Public State Banks

A second critical strategy to end Wall Street as we know it is to form 50 public state banks on the model of the Bank of North Dakota. These would function as real banks rather than the rigged casinos that pass for banks on Wall Street. State banks are designed to support community banks that, in turn, lend to local businesses. Most importantly, the public bankers would be paid reasonable salaries rather than gouging themselves at the trough. (See "Why is Socialism doing so darn well in Deep Red North Dakota?")

The Public Banking Institute is paving the way as its leaders (Ellen Brown and Marc Armstrong) help some 20 states explore the idea. They need and deserve our support. And for all you Fed haters, they also are formulating some very cool ideas about how to dramatically transform our central bank. (More on that in a future piece.) Most importantly, we all need to find a common way to protest Wall Street's rule over the economy and over Washington. This isn't about redistributing their wealth. It's about getting ours back.

Well, this certainly is a lot to chew on. It's hard to believe that the well-off would work so hard to make sure that you're not so well off. Perhaps having the states have their own banks might not be such a bad way to go. On the other hand, sometimes even the local banks can be a problem.

In the event that you still have any doubt that the Recovery you're experiencing may not feel all that uplifting, then this article by Nelson D. Schwartz should make it clear to you that recovering is substantially more difficult than getting into trouble in the first place. Getting us into trouble actually turned out to be a pretty darned good deal for those who got us in trouble in the first place. Now, as fate would have it, it seems as though this Recovery that we're in is also benefitting those who helped to get us into this mess to begin with. Is this a great country or what?

The Middle Class Is Steadily Eroding.
Just Ask the Business World.

By <u>NELSON D. SCHWARTZ</u> FEB. 2, 2014

In Manhattan, the upscale clothing retailer Barneys will replace the bankrupt discounter Loehmann's, whose Chelsea store closes in a few weeks. Across the country, Olive Garden and Red Lobster restaurants are struggling while fine-dining chains like Capital Grille are thriving. And at General Electric, the increase in demand for high-end dishwashers and refrigerators dwarfs sales growth of mass-market models.

As politicians and pundits in Washington continue to spar over whether economic inequality is in fact deepening, in corporate America there really is no debate at all. The post-recession reality is that the customer base for businesses that appeal to the middle class is shrinking as the top tier pulls even further away.

If there is any doubt, the speed at which companies are adapting to the new consumer landscape serves as very convincing evidence. Within top consulting firms and among Wall Street analysts, the shift is being described with a frankness more often associated with left-wing academics than business experts.

[150]

More at the Top

The top 5 percent of earners accounted for almost 40 percent of personal consumption expenditures in 2012, up from 27 percent in 1992. Largely driven by this increase, consumption among the top 20 percent grew to more than 60 percent over the same period.

Source: Institute for New Economic Thinking

"Those consumers who have capital like real estate and stocks and are in the top 20 percent are feeling pretty good," said John G. Maxwell, head of the global retail and consumer practice at PricewaterhouseCoopers.

In response to the upward shift in spending, PricewaterhouseCoopers clients, like big stores and restaurants, are chasing richer customers with a wider offering of high-end goods and services, or focusing on rock-bottom prices to attract the expanding ranks of penny-pinching consumers.

"As a retailer or restaurant chain, if you're not at the really high level or the low level, that's a tough place to be," Mr. Maxwell said. "You don't want to be stuck in the middle."

Although data on consumption is less readily available than figures that show a comparable split in income gains, new research by the economists Steven Fazzari, of Washington University in St. Louis, and Barry Cynamon, of the Federal Reserve Bank of St. Louis, backs up what is already apparent in the marketplace.

In 2012, the top 5 percent of earners were responsible for 38 percent of domestic consumption, up from 28 percent in 1995, the researchers found.

Even more striking, the current recovery has been driven almost entirely by the upper crust, according to Mr. Fazzari and Mr.

Cynamon. Since 2009, the year the recession ended, inflation-adjusted spending by this top echelon has risen 17 percent, compared with just 1 percent among the bottom 95 percent.

More broadly, about 90 percent of the overall increase in inflation-adjusted consumption between 2009 and 2012 was generated by the top 20 percent of households in terms of income, according to the study, which was sponsored by the Institute for New Economic Thinking, a research group in New York.

The effects of this phenomenon are now rippling through one sector after another in the American economy, from retailers and restaurants to hotels, casinos and even appliance makers.

For example, luxury gambling properties like Wynn and the Venetian in Las Vegas are booming, drawing in more high rollers than regional casinos in Atlantic City, upstate New York and Connecticut, which attract a less affluent clientele who are not betting as much, said Steven Kent, an analyst at Goldman Sachs.

Among hotels, revenue per room in the high-end category, which includes brands like the Four Seasons and St. Regis, grew 7.5 percent in 2013, compared with a 4.1 percent gain for midscale properties like Best Western, according to Smith Travel Research.

While spending among the most affluent consumers has managed to propel the economy forward, the sharpening divide is worrying, Mr. Fazzari said.

"It's going to be hard to maintain strong economic growth with such a large proportion of the population falling behind," he said. "We might be able to muddle along — but can we really recover?"

Mr. Fazzari also said that depending on a relatively small but affluent slice of the population to drive demand makes the economy more volatile, because this group does more discretionary spending that can rise and fall with the stock market, or track seesawing housing prices. The run-up on Wall Street in recent years has only heightened these trends, said Guy Berger, an economist at RBS, who estimates that 50 percent of Americans have no effective participation in the surging stock market, even counting retirement accounts.

Regardless, affluent shoppers like Mitchell Goldberg, an independent investment manager in Dix Hills, N.Y., say the rising stock market has encouraged people to open their wallets and purses more.

"Opulence isn't back, but we're spending a little more comfortably," Mr. Goldberg said. He recently replaced his old Nike golf clubs with Callaway drivers and Adams irons, bought a Samsung tablet for work, and traded in his minivan for a sport utility vehicle.

And while the superrich garner much of the attention, most companies are building their business strategies around a broader slice of affluent consumers.

At G.E. Appliances, for example, the fastest-growing brand is the Café line, which is aimed at the top quarter of the market, with refrigerators typically retailing for $1,700 to $3,000.

"This is a person who is willing to pay for features, like a double-oven range or a refrigerator with hot water," said Brian McWaters, a general manager in G.E.'s Appliance division.
At street level, the divide is even more stark.

Sears and J. C. Penney, retailers whose wares are aimed squarely at middle-class Americans, are both in dire straits. Last month, Sears said it would shutter its flagship store on State Street in downtown Chicago, and J. C. Penney announced the closings of 33 stores and 2,000 layoffs.

Loehmann's, where generations of middle-class shoppers hunted for marked-down designer labels in the famed Back Room, is now being liquidated after three trips to bankruptcy court since 1999.

The Loehmann's store in Chelsea, like all 39 Loehmann's outlets nationwide, will go dark as soon as the last items sell. Barneys New York, which started in the same location in 1923 before moving to a more luxurious spot on Madison Avenue two decades ago, plans to reopen a store on the site in 2017.

Investors have taken notice of the shrinking middle. Shares of Sears and J. C. Penney have fallen more than 50 percent since the end of 2009, even as upper-end stores like Nordstrom and bargain-basement chains like Dollar Tree and Family Dollar Stores have more than doubled in value over the same period. Competition from online giants like Amazon has only added to the problems faced by old-line retailers, of course. But changes in the restaurant business show that the effects of rising inequality are widespread.

A shift at Darden, which calls itself the world's largest full-service restaurant owner, encapsulates the trend. Foot traffic at mid-tier, casual dining properties like Red Lobster and Olive Garden has dropped in every quarter but one since 2005, according to John Glass, a restaurant industry analyst at Morgan Stanley.

With diners paying an average tab of $16.50 a person at Olive Garden, Mr. Glass said, "The customers are middle class. They're not rich. They're not poor." With income growth stagnant and prices for necessities like health care and education on the rise, he said, "They are cutting back." On the other hand, at the Capital Grille, an upscale Darden chain where the average check per person is about $71, spending is up by an average of 5 percent annually over the last three years.

LongHorn Steakhouse, another Darden chain, has been reworked to target a slightly more affluent crowd than Olive Garden, with décor intended to evoke a cattleman's ranch instead of an Old West theme.

Now, hedge fund investors are pressuring Darden's management to break up the company and spin out the more upscale properties into a separate entity.

"A separation could make sense from a strategic perspective," Mr. Glass said. "Generally, the specialty restaurant group is more attractive demographically."

Now, all of this informative data is designed to do what? Help you to better understand what you already know, which is that you're getting porked. By "getting porked", we do not mean to imply that someone will be arriving at your home with a truckload of bacon. No, it means that you're getting boned, screwed, taken advantage of, or as we like to say here in Vermont, fucked.

This Recovery is hitting you like a freight train and you never even saw it coming. It's not like this is your fault, by the way. It's hard to see a train coming when you're blindfolded and those tying on the blindfold are telling you that the train you're hearing is on another set of tracks and that you need not worry. I know what you're thinking. You're thinking, "Why is it in the best interest of the very rich to eliminate the Middle Class and ruin all those great American businesses referenced in that article above?"

You see, you're much smarter than you think you are just for having a mind curious enough to ask that question. It is a real

[155]

head-scratcher when you think about it. It would stand to reason that having a strong, stable Middle Class, much like what we had when I was kid growing up in the '50s, would make for a much stronger and more stable country. Sure, we've always had some rich folks around and it was a darned good thing that we did, too. It was the handful of rich folks that helped to keep the locals employed year-round back in a time when there wasn't a whole lot to do here in Vermont. I'm talking about back before skiing. Yes, there was a time that people did not come here to ski. Actually, they did not come here at all except perhaps to get away from where they were, which had to be pretty bad if this place looked good to them.

If you want to know the answer to your question, you need only to look at Haiti. Here's a country that has no Middle Class. They have a whole lot of really, really poor people and a tiny group of really, really rich people. That country works great, don't you think? Oh, you don't agree? Well, that's too bad, because that appears to be where our Recovery is leading us, so it might be beneficial for you to brush up on your "yessah Master" so that you can be better prepared for the new fun times headed your way. It may work to your advantage to find a way to suck up to those who are on the road to owning you. Your other choice, risky at best and most likely fatal, is to fight back. That, of course, would take balls. If you choose this option it might behoove you join up with a group of disgruntled Vermonters. If you have any doubt of the success of this option, I would encourage you to go have a discussion with General Pickett.

CHAPTER 13

Hanging by a Nose as Opposed to a Thread

To better prepare you for you bleak future under the glorious Recovery that is destined to benefit about 15 people at the expense of around $300 million or so others, you might care to know how others deal with adversity and trauma so that you, too will know how to respond when the day comes when you find yourself hanging by your nose.

In the summer of 1957, there wasn't much happening in the life of the average six year old Vermonter. The most exciting thing that had not yet happened was the debut of "Leave it to Beaver" starring Jerry Matthews. That show began in October. Our excitement began earlier that summer on one of those hot, sticky summer days that you remember for the rest of your life. Days like these are made more memorable if and when something remarkable (and not necessarily in a good way) happens to your best friend.

We'll call my childhood friend Tom, as he's still alive and there's no need to go looking for litigation if we can avoid it. Tom and I were inseparable as kids. We did everything together, not that there was ever much to do. We never had any money when we were six years old, which was perfect because there was nothing to buy anyway. There was Annie Jewel's store about a mile down the road and we would walk down there once in a while, but more just to see what was happening at Annie Jewel's store. If we had a penny or two, we might get a couple of pieces of penny candy, like a Tootsie Roll or something, but more often than not we'd just sit around and watch Annie, and her husband Ernie Jewel, just putter around. Watching two adults puttering around their store qualified as something to do in 1957. It was more of something to do than the nothing to do at our own homes.

Today, on this hot summer day, things were different. We did have something to do. My older brother, Jim, Tom and I decided that we were going to go over the bank and hang out. The back yard of my parents place was flat as a pancake until it wasn't. When you went back about 150 feet, the ground dropped right off at about a 30% grade for about 150 feet before it flattened back out again slid into the West Branch of the Battenkill River. We ruined many a pair of pants sliding down the bank.

The top of the bank, or the end of our yard, served as a deserted rail bed that once had the Manchester, Dorset, and Granville (New York), or MD&G as it was known, travel over it carrying lord knows what; probably marble. The tracks were long gone, but on the days when we exhibited great drive and ambition and felt like digging, we could generally turn up a railroad spike or two. Once, we did find an arrowhead. That gave us great pause as we fantasized Indians attacking the train and stealing their.....marble? Well, OK, it didn't really matter because at that age and at that time playing "Cowboys and Indians" was a favorite pastime and we had no problem visualizing the Indians jumping all over the slow-moving train.

But today was not the day for playing Cowboys and Indians. It was a day for doing nothing at all. It was too freakin' hot to bother. The only place to be was down at our makeshift fort, over the bank and fairly near the cool river. We spent some time scoping out for frogs that might be crazy enough to lie around on the banks of the river. For six year old Vermont kids with nothing to do, frogs, unfortunately, were fair game. Now I'm not saying that killing frogs is a good thing and it was never anything I thought teaching my kids about was a good idea, but it was, for whatever reason, just something we did. Today, I guess kids kill each other. They'd be better off takin' out a frog or two. The sensation is about the same, but penalty is a whole lot less severe. Frogs were pretty sneaky and quick, too - especially for a six year old. They weren't generally in any great danger and trying to catch them got old quick. We didn't have the tolerance or patience. Those were traits that came with age. We didn't have much age going on either.

Remember when you were that age? It would seem like whatever your best friend would do was hysterical even if it wasn't. Things seemed more alive and important back then, probably because there was no other benchmark. If you didn't know any better (and lord knows we most certainly didn't), you would think that having your best friend damn near tear his nose off would be THE funniest thing you had ever seen to date, but that would primarily be because you were so young as to not have seen all that many funny things. Time not only heals all wounds. It also provides you with other benchmarks for what is and is not funny.

We had spent quite a while doing our "Lord of the Flies" thing with the frogs; not that we knew anything about that book, mind you. It was published about three years prior to this day and we weren't at that reading level yet anyway. That book might very well have been written about life growing up in Vermont, but probably not. We were slightly nicer to each other.

The frog hunting had become passé. It was too much work on this hot day so we decided to go back to our fort. Having zero resources, it would have been difficult for the untrained eye to determine the area where we had staked our claim as an actual fort. There was a couple of old cement blocks that we had found that had been tossed over the bank most likely after they did the foundation to my parent's house. Nice thing about having a bank is that you have a convenient place to throw stuff that you no longer need, like extra cement blocks. Resources being as scarce as they were, very little went to waste. This was especially true when you had about a dozen neighborhood kids running around always looking to scarf up whatever might be of value to use for their fort. A cement block was a real commodity and in extremely short supply. If you had a cement block to sit on versus an uneven, moss-covered rock to sit on, it would save you from tons of humiliation. Sitting on a moss-covered rock will inevitably leave a big ol' wet spot on the back of your pants, which will result in having your friends cry out that you shit your pants. Now you can argue all you want that it's just a wet spot from sitting on a moss-covered rock, but there's no way you're winning the argument.

Since my brother was three years older than Tom and me, and substantially heavier and stronger, and since we only had the one cement block, I ended up sitting on a moss-covered rock. I knew the ramifications of doing so, but I also knew that I had no other options. As it turned out there was one other option.

I could've done what Tom did which was to climb up into a dwarfed apple tree that had a nearly horizontal branch extending back towards the bank. The branch was just barely big enough so that Tom could stretch out and lie there pretty comfortably as long as he didn't move anything more than an eyelash.

"Man, that's a pretty slick place to sit. I wish I had thought of that." I thought to myself. As has often proven to be the case throughout my life, it pays not to be too smart. Here was my brother, Jim, perched on the cement block most likely feeling like King Tut or something, and to some degree rightfully so, since it was the only cement block and did take on a bit of a regal aura about it. There I was feeling the back of my pants getting damper with each passing minute but not really giving a shit because I had already planned to be the last one crawling back up the bank when it was time to go home so that the other two would not see the emerging wet spot on my jeans and holler out loud enough so Annie Jewel could hear "Hey, look. Bobby shit his pants."

I had hedged my bets. There's ol' Tom lying on the apple branch big as can be. He looked like a lion or some other big cat. He was always a little on the pudgy side; sort of like my brother, Jim. I looked more like someone from a refugee camp that hadn't seen food in a few months. Blonde hair, blue eyes, white skin and bones. That was me. Had I been the one in the tree things might have been very different. Light as I was, I may have very well been hanging there for days before my nose split.

When it was time to come home, our mom, Thyra, would bang on the large silver bell that hung outside our house. We never

[161]

gave any of this two thoughts, but it is hard to imagine today that there was a time when you would let your kids out, much like Jim the Farmer would let out his cows for the day, let them roam around unattended for almost the entire day and then call them back for dinner. There were days that we'd pack a peanut butter and jelly sandwich, along with some other treats, and head off up the mountain. We'd be gone all day but would always come home for dinner. It was not because we were told to. It was mostly because we didn't want to spend the night in the woods with nothing but the crust of our peanut butter and jelly sandwich, which you would only eat if stranded overnight in the woods with nothing else to eat.

You could hear the bell from a long ways away. The entire neighborhood knew when the Stannard family was having dinner. Today was going to be no exception. The bell's tone resonated throughout the cool forest where we had sought respite for an entire day. We didn't do much, because there wasn't much to do. It didn't matter, even a little bit, because we were, in spite of the rampant boredom, having a pretty good time. Little did we know that our pretty good time was about take a turn for the hysterical; for two of us anyway.

"Guess we better get going" said Jim. "Ma doesn't like us being late." She knew we were down the bank and at best, would ring that bell three times. Any more than three rings and there would be hell to pay. We never thought much about this at the time, but apparently as long as your kids were within three loud bell rings away, all was right with the world. If you had to ring the bell four or five times, I guess that meant trouble for the parents. The only thing that would have saved our lives would be that if we were somehow nearly dead out in the woods and the crows were already starting to pick away at us. If we were late, because we were just dickin' around, watch out. Thyra was part Swedish (the nice part) and part German (the not so nice part; the German part we figured ran the camps during WWII. Don't mess with the German part). Life was always much better if you played into the Swedish part. Unfortunately, my brother, Jim, and I played into her German part more often than not.

Today was going to be one of the days that we would not make it home by the third bell. Today was one of the days where we were going to risk dealing with the German side. We hoped and prayed that the reason for our delay would hold up in the Court of Thyra. If not, we were doomed.

Jim relinquished his rights to the cement block and started walking towards the three boulders that had been left behind as the result of the glacier that once covered the back yards of Vermont. At the time, the boulders seemed huge. They all rested against each other like they had been carefully placed there by some giant. I was skinny enough so that I could slither in between them, not that there was any real advantage to doing so.

Knowing the back of my pants were wet and subject to great ridicule I was intentionally taking my time getting up off the moss-covered rock. It was no doubt going to be in my best interest to wait a second and let Tom come down out of the tree before I got up and showed off my wet butt and be forced to listen to the howls of laughter about the faux shit stains. I rose very slowly; careful to keep my backside from the view of the other two. At the same time I was getting up, Tom was beginning his decent out of the tree.

As everything did back then because we were small, this tree looked big. It wasn't really. As is generally the case, getting up in a tree is a lot easier than getting down out of one. This is especially true if you've been lying extremely still, not moving anything but an occasional eyelash or two, for fear of falling out of the tree. His not yet fully developed muscles had stiffened up pretty good. He swung one leg over; then the other. The smart play would have been to jump, but I can appreciate why he didn't as it was just high enough that he probably thought he was going to die. Dying would have been better than what did happen.

Tom reached around and grabbed the tree and started to let himself sort of slide down the trunk. Hmm, not a bad exit plan. He slowly slid down the trunk until his feet were just about two inches from the ground. He was just about home free, until he wasn't.

As he let go of the trunk of the tree to fall the last couple of inches he stopped dead in mid-air. He immediately started yelling, which caused my brother to turn around. I shifted to make darned sure he couldn't see the wet spot on my pants while my eyes were riveted to the scene unfolding before me.

My best friend was hanging from an apple by his nose. Now, for those of you unfamiliar with apple trees, they are cousins of the thorn apple tree. The thorn apple tree has long, protruding thorns that are as sharp as any needle. Getting too close to a thorn apple tree always spells trouble. You're going to get stabbed no matter how careful you are.

The apple tree, however, thankfully does not have two-inch spears growing out of its branches. Instead it has smaller, mutant nubs about one-half to three-quarters of an inch long. They are not sharp, but they are sturdy. Sturdy enough to hold fast while a chubby, six year old kid dangles away with his nose securely stuck on one of the protruding nubs. He hung there for about ten eternities, or so it seemed.

His arms were flailing and he was hollering up a storm. There was nothing we could do except to try and keep from wetting our pants at this unbelievable display of tissue strength. Now, I'm not saying that this was funny, because hanging by your nose from an apple tree with your feet just barely, but not quite, touching the ground with your arms flailing away and you're oh so close to the ground feet kicking away is really not funny. But when you're six years old and your best friend is hanging by his nose from an apple tree with his feet just barely, but not quite, touching the ground with his feet kicking away and he's screaming bloody murder, I'm sorry but it's freakin' hilarious.

One thousand one….one thousand two….one thousand…..RIP. I don't care how light you are, your nose is no contest up against a nub of an apple tree. Those nubs have gone through thousands of years of evolution to make sure that they are some tough and they are not about to give in to some six year old kid who has decided to hook his nostril over the nub and dangle there for a while. Nosiree, the nub is not giving in. The nose, on the other hand, has not had the benefit of evolution to prepare it for this level of stress and tension. Uh uh. It was the nose that called it a day. Left with no choice, the right side of his right nostril separated from his face causing three things to happen simultaneously.

First, Tom came crashing to the ground and placed his hands over his face.

Next, blood began to flow. Oh baby, we're talking the nosebleed from hell. We had no way of knowing that there would be a time when there would be a movie released called "The Texas Chainsaw Massacre" in which there might have been a little more blood than what we were witnessing, but not much more. Oh man, what a mess.

Third, as hard as Jim and I tried to help poor nose-detached-from-face Tom, we just couldn't move from where we were. There may have been something in the world funnier to two brothers six and nine years of age than seeing their friend dangling from an apple tree by his surrendering, now profusely bleeding nose, but if there was, we'd not yet seen it. Maybe watching someone getting covered with putrid cow parts from an exploding cow could top this, but that would be in the eyes of the beholder. Come to think of it, that's about where we were here.

Tom was oh so very sincerely not amused at our laughter which had the unfortunate reaction of causing my brother and I to laugh even more uncontrollably; if that was even possible.

"Neejus Christ...dnis isn't 'unking 'unny you 'ssholes. I 'orn off my 'unking nose."

Well, if the unfortunate occurrence of catching your nose on a stub of an apple tree wasn't funny enough, that response just about caused the two of us to stop breathing. Jim finally said, "Keep pressure on it and let's get up to the house."

Shit, the house. Thyra was on her 5th or 6th ring by now. We couldn't possibly let Tom go home by himself. Oh no, we had to bring him home with us as living proof as to why we were late. If not, there would be much more blood spilt here today.

The three of us climbed up the steep bank; gravel slipping and sliding under our respective feet. We were all praying that Tom didn't slip. We didn't have the moral fortitude to survive another cataclysmic, humorous event today. We made it to the house where Thyra was angrily awaiting our arrival. Her anger turned to horror when she saw the blood.

"What on earth happened?" she demanded. I could feel the urge of uncontrollable laughter welling up inside of me. I knew if I opened my mouth that I would begin laughing hysterically and by doing so, would lead to Thyra killing me dead on the spot, because, as you know, this was not a funny situation. I looked at Jim praying that he would take the initiative. His eyes gave him away. He, too, was confronting the pressure of hysterical laughter welling up inside of him. As a result, we both stood there like frozen statues squeezing every muscle in our body in hopes that neither of us cracked a smile, because had we done so, we were goners.

"I 'ore my 'ose off on ah apple 'ree" Tom said.

Neither Jim nor I were ever very good at things like church-going and/or praying, but believe me at this moment in time I was begging the lord to give me strength; strength to stand there and not move one fucking muscle for fear of exploding like the aforementioned cow in chapter 6.

"We've got to get you cleaned up and get you home right now." said Thyra, with the voice of authority that remained with her until the day she died.

She escorted Tom into the house. I held back for one-half of a second and let Jim go on ahead. There was no way I was going to let him see the wet spot on the back of my pants for which I would have had no defense.

It took some time, about a decade or so for Tom to fully recover. Oh, his nose healed up fairly quickly considering how severe a wound it was. I'm not sure it was ever even stitched back together. I seem to think they just taped it or something. Either way, it did heal. It was tough seeing him for a while after that. Laughter is one powerful reflex and just when you think you've got a grip on it, BANG, you don't. Back it comes just like when it first started. It took while, a long while, but there came a time when even Tom thought that hanging by his nose from an apple tree with his feet almost, but not quite, touching the ground did have an element of humor about it.

"Not as funny as you shitting your pants, though" he said.

No defense was forthcoming.

CHAPTER 14

Burnin' Down the House

Thus far, we've learned that we've gone through a Recession that was designed to cost you everything you own and now we're going through a Recovery that is designed to ensure that you don't ever get any of what you lost back. None of this was really any of your doing, notwithstanding the greed that you exhibited when you were up there in the clouds with the 1% just prior to losing all you own, because you thought a guy named Bernie Madoff would do you right.

It's hard to imagine any native Vermonter investing money, as they don't have any to invest. However, even if they did have some to invest, it's hard to imagine a native Vermonter investing their incredibly hard earned money with a guy named Made-OFF. Something about Made-OFF and money in the same sentence would, in all likelihood, be sending up just about every hackle any self-respecting Vermonter might have. We didn't fight through God knows how many wars, and how many more mosquitos, just to be taken in by someone with an inspirational last name. We learned a long time ago that when it comes to making money pigs get fat and hogs get slaughtered.

If those last words of wisdom are causing you to scratch your head, it's no wonder you're broke. The deck is stacked against you and unless you can figure out how to be the dealer (good luck with that), then you're much better off trying figure out how you can be the guy working in the coat check room. You're not going to end up at the top, but if you play your cards right, you might end up somewhere and not wearing chains.

No one ever said this Recovery business was going to be easy. Of course, they never told you that there would be people that we elected to look out for us who spend most of their time not looking out for us. So, that's just another exit blocked by fire.

What you need is a hose. Well, a hose and some minor understanding on how to use it. Hoses come in handy when the house is on fire as I would learn the hard way. It was the year that the smoke detector created by Malcolm Cooper, Sr. started a fire that damned near burned his house down.

The alarm rang and the radio devices that let people know there's an emergency were going off. There was a fire at the Cooper residence in Dorset Hollow. Technically, it was on the corner of Dorset Hollow Road and the road that went to Kirby Hollow. The road came in from Rt. 30 and headed east before it forked and went right, up into Dorset Hollow or left, towards Kirby Hollow. The house was perched up on a little hill overlooking the beginnings of the Mettowee River which flowed under the Dorset Hollow Road just before the bend turning right. It was a fortuitous place for a fire as the river was right there at the bottom of the hill. All the fire trucks would be able to set pumps into the river and pump hundreds of gallons of water on the house fire.

The best laid plans.

Whenever there was a fire in Dorset, one of two people arrived at the Dorset Fire House first. It was either Ray Bushee or Austin Rumney who would arrive first. The reasons were simple. Ray lived right in town, just up the street from the Fire House. He drove a taxi cab, which looking back must have been a strange occupation inasmuch as nobody was going anywhere. He also drove the school bus. He was a great bus driver until he wasn't. Ray could be a bit of a prick with his plaid porkpie hat and his stubby cigar. He was a tough guy. The last place in the world you would want your eyes to fall would be on the mirror secured to his visor on the bus. It seemed like every time I ever looked up into that mirror, there would be Ray's piercing eyes starring right back at me saying, "Don't even fucking think about it", in which case I would immediately stop thinking altogether.

Ray was noted for driving like Parnelli Jones from his house on Rt. 30 to the Fire House. Then, once he got inside the fire truck, something happened. No one ever knew or said anything, but once Ray got in the truck time slowed way down. I oftentimes thought that he so enjoyed the moments when he got the chance to get out of his black taxi cab into that fire engine red fire engine that he just wanted to savor the experience forever. I'm sure you could appreciate the excitement that this provided to an otherwise fairly mundane life. That is, unless it was your house that was on fire.

Fortunately for Mr. Cooper, Austin beat Ray to the Fire House this time. Austin owned and operated H.N. Williams Department Store, which was conveniently located adjacent to the Fire House. By rights, Austin should have been the first responder on every fire but presumably he would be counting out change while Ray "Parnelli Jones" Bushee was racing to get to the Fire House first. On those occasions, Ray would beat out Austin. On the day of Mr. Cooper's fire, there was no change to be counted out and Austin beat Ray to the station. He hopped in the first available truck and off he went. It was up to the other Firemen to meet him at the fire.

Everyone knew where the Cooper house was so this was not as odd as it may seem. Generally speaking, you would wait until other firemen showed up and leave with a crew. There was no crew today; just Austin and the fire engine.

He turned right into Dorset Hollow and arrived at the intersection of the two roads. He had to be thinking on his way to the fire that his best bet would be to get a pump in that river and get volumes of water up to the house, and he was right in his thinking. However, he was wrong in the implementation.

For reasons that no one but Austin would ever know (he opted never to share his thoughts with anyone even long after the house had been rebuilt. Plus, it was never really a good idea to ask Austin, or anyone for that matter, why they made what appeared to be a bit of a bad decision. It was just bad form), he parked the fire engine right across the Dorset Hollow Road. He jumped out, set the pump in the river and got water to the hose instantly.

That was the good news. The bad news was that once the road was completely blocked no other trucks could get by. It was one of the damned if you do, damned if you don't situations. To move the truck now would mean that the pump would have to be pulled from the river and thus the water would stop flowing to the fire; OR leave things as they were, turn the numerous other trucks around and drive all the way around through Dorset onto to Peace Street onto Kirby Hollow Road and all the way back around to the Cooper house. That appeared to be the best option.

At one point I found myself inside the house with Mr. Cooper. Water was flying right along with the sparks.

"Can you give me a hand with this piano?" he asked.

Now, I had taken piano lessons when I was younger but I didn't think that this was any time for a concert. This was a grand piano that weighed slightly more than the largest block of marble at the Dorset Quarry. I could maybe carry the bench.

"Where would you like to go with it?" I asked, nervously

"Let's get it outside."

"Yes, let's."

Thankfully, at this precise moment, about four or five big, giant guys showed up. We all grabbed onto to a piece of the huge piano and marched right out through the French doors. There was little concern for hitting the door trim. Miraculously, we were able to get the piano out on the lawn.

The roar of the flames were dwarfed by the bitching and yelling directed at Austin for parking the first fire engine on the scene diagonally across the road so nobody else could get in or out. Ray's voice could be heard well above the din.

"If you had waited and let me take the first truck, this wouldn't have happened. I'd never park a truck like that..." bellowed Ray.

"Probably not." replied Austin calmly; never one known for wasting words.

In spite of the somewhat controversial parking job that ended up being the talk of the town for most of the next few months and notwithstanding a gallant effort to do otherwise, the firemen were able to save the house.

At the next firemen's meeting, there was much consternation and dialog about protocol when arriving on the scene and not blocking major roads. The bitching and moaning was obviously all directed at Austin but you couldn't tell by looking at him. He sat right there staring straight ahead just like he was in church or something. The harsh words rolled off him like water off a duck.

After all the gum-flapping had finally subsided, the room became silent. Silence was a place where Austin always felt pretty comfortable; not that anyone else did. After a long time had passed, the silence was broken.

"We saved the place." was all he said.

Now the track record for saving houses on fire anywhere is usually pretty small. In Dorset the motto was "We never lost a cellar hole yet."

It's hard to argue with success. Let that be a lesson to you.

CHAPTER 15

The Prank

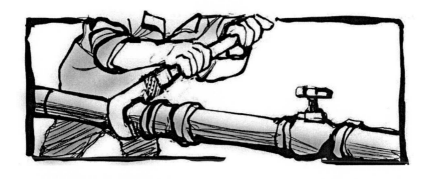

As you are beginning to learn, there's more than one way to skin a cat (or bury an exploding cow or deal with a runaway mouse). Surviving an economic recovery that, in all likelihood, will not benefit you even a little bit presents the opportunity for a weak individual, such as yourself, to fall into a state of complete disrepair. When reality sets in, it has the unfortunate consequence of being real.

You were sitting there one minute pondering about how things actually seemed like they were getting better and dreaming about the life you once had until you dropped like a rock tossed into a quarry. Then, without notice, they shut off your heat. How's that Recovery working out for you? Don't worry, if you've played your cards right and made a few Vermont friends, they won't let you freeze to death. Vermonters take their heat pretty seriously, since it's winter here for about ten months a year followed by two months of fairly chilly days.

Compared to what some Vermonters have had to endure, freezing to death would be considered a welcome respite. "What the hell could possibly be worse than freezing to death, you asshole?" I can hear you screaming.

First off, keep your voice down. There's no need to get all riled up. There are things much worse than death; freezing or otherwise. For instance, living. OK, let's clarify that a little. Living after your wife discovered what she thought was a used condom in your lunchbox. This is especially precarious if your wife happens to be insanely jealous of you.

"Hell, I'm more likely to freeze to death than to have that ever happen to me." you say. Not so fast there, Buddy. Maybe you're not as plugged in to Vermont life as we had thought.

My dad was a seventh generation Vermonter and the son of a bootlegger-turned-plumber. He was the middle child of five children. If you know anything at all about kids, you know that the middle child, generally speaking, is the one completely

[176]

ignored by the parents. The first child is doted on morning and night until he or she grows up, at which time he/she is then responsible for each and every ill that befalls the other children.

Then you have the middle child; what middle child?

Then you have the youngest sibling who can never, ever do anything wrong, because that child is the parent's link to youth. That poor creature will be the "Baby of the Family" for all times. That sucker can be sixty years old and his mother eighty-two and mom will still be talking baby talk to him. Tragic, yes, but it's just the way it is.

There were four boys and one girl in my dad's family. It's a wonder they even knew he, my dad, was in the family. There was a time when he was around thirteen or so that he decided to play what in later years he would become nearly famous for, a prank. He was friends with Gib Mack of Pawlet. Those two boys were identical twins from different families. After hanging out together for a Saturday, when it was time to go home, they decided to go home to the other's family. The story goes that neither parents noticed until the next day. Middle kids from a white family could probably change families and show up at a black family's house and still not be noticed for a day or two.

Perhaps it's this lack of attention that causes middle kids to be different from their older and/or younger siblings. Who knows? This book is not designed to be an aid for those in need of a psychoanalyst's services. We're trying to help your sorry ass survive a Recovery; such as it is, and the best, if not maybe the only way you're going to get through this crisis, is to have a few extra tools in your toolbox of life. Surviving the prank of all pranks might just be that one tool that could make all the difference. Here's hoping.

It was around the summer of 1967. The irony is not lost on us today that the Doors, "Light My Fire" and the Beatles, "All You

Need is Love", topped the charts that year. Oh, if those boys only knew.

My dad spent most of his working life with Ken Nichols. The tales that have come in over the years of the antics between these two men is the stuff of legends. By this time, my dad and his brother owned the plumbing company along with their mom. His father had passed leaving the plumbing business to the three of them. Years later, that unfortunate decision would be the cause of an irreconcilable family split, but oh well. Shit happens.

Almost every day, at some point during the day, my father would bet Ken a dollar over something ridiculous. Ken would nearly always lose. Not unlike a visit to Las Vegas, he would win just enough to keep him coming back for more. Here's a very small example of the kind thing we're talking about.

The two of them were in a basement in one of the old, stately houses of Manchester Village replacing a line for an old steam boiler. This was labor intensive work, which meant that Ken was very busy, as my dad wasn't known for killing himself on the job. Two inch iron pipe had to be cut by hand and both ends had to be threaded by hand. Then pipe dope (my how those two words have taken on an entirely different meaning over the past 45 years or so) would be applied to the newly threaded ends and screwed into a fitting of some sort. To tighten the pipe securely they would use 24" long, red, cast metal pipe wrenches. They weighed a ton and if you weren't really strong when you started a job like this. you were by the time it was finished. Ken was already very strong.

Some would refer to Kenny as a bull because he really was one of the strongest guys on any crew. He was short and stocky with short cut hair thicker than any bristle doormat. His arms were the size of my legs. Fortunately, he was one of the best natured souls that ever walked the face of the earth. Oh sure, if you got a little whiskey into him, he could get rowdy with the best of

[178]

them, but I don't think there was a person alive who ever saw him get really mad or lose his shit. Good thing, too because boy, there would be hell to pay.

Ken had two, two-foot long, red pipe wrenches; one in each hand. I could pick one of those up with two hands no problem. One wrench was on the end of a union fitting designed to allow two pieces of pipe to be secured in a continuous line. The other wrench was on the pipe. Ken was pulling the wrenches in the opposite direction thus tightening the two pieces together. Sweat was pouring off his head as he worked on the two wrenches.

He had about pulled his guts out when my father asked, "Are you going to tighten those?"

Ken stopped grunting long enough to look at my father with a most puzzled expression, "What?"

"I said are you going to stop fucking around and tighten those fittings up. We don't have all day." Big Jim (as he was known) said.

"What the hell are you talking about?" said Ken. "That's as tight as those sons-a-bitches are gonna get!"

"I'll bet you a dollar I can turn that pipe a full turn." my father challenged. It might be helpful to know that although my father was pretty rugged in his own right; his strength was no match for Ken. Not even close. I recall standing there somewhat befuddled. I could tell by the way the veins in Ken's neck were nearly exploding that this pipe was about as tight as humanly possible. I couldn't imagine anyone, nonetheless my dad, taking that another turn. Maybe he'd lost his mind. That was entirely possible as he did have a history of doing some rather crazy things. Or maybe today was the day that he was going to let Kenny win one. Either way this was sure to be exciting (this more than qualifies for excitement in Vermont).

[179]

Ken almost sprained his wrist trying to get a dollar out of his pocket. He slammed the dollar down on the dirt floor in the crawl space where we were working. "You might just as well as give me your dollar right now, 'cause I'm telling you, that pipe ain't movin' a smidgen; say nothin' about a full turn." Ken said with a touch of defiance in his voice.

Big Jim confidently took a dollar bill out of his pocket and laid it carefully on top of Ken's dollar on the dirt floor. "Give me those wrenches." my father commanded in his best 2nd Lieutenant voice. Ken eagerly surrendered his grip on the wrenches. My dad looked at me and gave me a wink as he removed the wrenches from the pipe, reversed them, and backed the pipe off one full turn. He let go of the wrenches and picked up the two, one dollar bills that were resting comfortably on the dirt floor.

"Hey, wait a minute…" Ken pleaded.

"I said I could turn them a full turn. I didn't say which way." said Big Jim as he stuffed the two bills in his right, hip pocket.

"Sum-a-bitch" Ken mumbled under his breath. I stared at the floor. The last thing I wanted to see was Ken's wrath directed my way. You know the old expression; "It's easier to kick the dog than the one you're mad at." No way was I going to be the dog.

That was just an example of the day-to-day life of these two characters. Suffice it to say that there was a bond between these men that could never be duplicated. They had fun. They had great respect for each other. They were employer and employee, but they were much more than that. They were damn near a comedy act on every job they were ever on. Ken was the straight man to whatever hideous thing my father would conjure up; and boy, could he conjure stuff up. As if he needed help (he didn't), this one day in 1967 would prove to be the prank of all pranks. Now, I'm not saying that this was a good prank or a good idea. I think the only thing one can say about this event is that, not unlike other dumb ideas that spring into people's heads (like mortgage backed derivatives), this prank might have benefitted from a little more time spent on the outcome.

As previously mentioned, Ken's wife, Jean, was, shall we say, rather jealous of Ken. They loved each other dearly, but Jean was one tough cookie and Ken knew better than to mess with her. Other than Ken, she had two boys, one of whom is currently serving as a Town Father of Manchester. Ken knew how Jean felt about him and also knew that if ever cheated on her, he might as well just kill himself when it was over; rather like one of those bees whose testicles explode after sex with a queen bee.

Yes, according to Neatorama, *"The reproductive cycle of bees is fascinating - and complex. But here's the short story: a queen is selectively bred in a special "queen cell" in the hive and fed royal jelly by worker bees to induce her to become sexually mature.*

A virgin queen that survives to adulthood without being killed by her rivals will take a mating flight with a dozen or so male drones (out of tens of thousands eligible bachelors in the colony). But don't call these drones lucky because during mating, their genitals explode and snap off inside the queen!"

This would be nothing compared to what Jean would do to Ken should Ken decide, in a moment of weakness, to take on another queen bee. Ken knew what his fate would be as did just about everyone else who ever knew either of them. Yessir, staying true was a much better deal than staying dead, which was why this particular prank was so egregious.

One of dad's best friends in the world was a man named Ed Tarbell (to learn more about Ed, I would recommend you get a copy of "How to Survive the Recession – A Vermont Perspective"). Ed was a true Vermonter and a character. He was a quiet sort of guy who kept his friends guessing as to just what was going on inside that head of his. Ed was a bit of a handful as a kid and was raised by his grandparents for fear that his parents might just kill him. Hey, we've all been there.

Ed's grandfather owned the West Side Market in Dorset. This place was always a mystery as it was located on the east side of Rt. 30. This particular day, Dad was called in to replace a sink in the back of the store. Of course, what this meant was that Ken would be fixing the sink in the back of the store while Ed and Big Jim played cards on the counter up towards the front of the store.

The two childhood friends played cards while Ken worked away happily in the back of the store. It rolled around to lunch time and all three sat down to eat lunch and of course play a round of cribbage. My dad played cards nearly every day. He'd play poker, pitch, cribbage, gin (he'd drink that, too) whatever anyone wanted to play. It didn't matter what the game was. He just loved playing cards. I think he was either psychic or a really good card counter, because inevitably at some point during a card game, when his opponent was about to lay down a card, he would ask, "Are you sure you want to put down the King of Spades?", which of course was the identical card that the person would have in their hand. He'd only do that once in a while, but he did it enough so that it was more than a little unnerving.

After lunch, which rarely lasted more than 30 minutes no matter how intense the card game was, it was time to go back to work. There were two distinctly different paths taken on this sunny afternoon. Ken went back to working on installing the new sink. Ed and Big Jim went to work on an idea that Ed had that Big Jim just couldn't resist. This idea might just end up with Ken being in the dog house for all eternity; and that would be if he was really lucky.

It's hard to believe it today, but there was a time when condoms were not on display. They had to be purchased with a wink and a nod from the person behind the counter. Today, of course, you can walk into any chain store pharmacy and you will see an entire section dedicated to all different brands of condoms, gels and maybe even sex toys. You and your kids can stand right there and gawk at ribbed condoms, lubricated condoms and colored condoms with about as much emotion and concern as if you were looking for eggs in the dairy aisle.

This is now; that was then. You could buy condoms in the '60s, but it helped if you knew the person behind the counter because that's where they were kept; far away from the curious eyes of kids and prissy wives. For reasons only these two, long dead, friends will ever know, they thought it would be a fun idea to sacrifice one of the condoms for something other than its intended purpose.

Ed tore open the package and fully extended the condom. While he was busy doing, this Big Jim was over in aisle three getting a glass bottle (they didn't use plastic bottles back then) of Jergen's Hand Lotion. With Ken busy whistling while he was working, these two demons were squirting some, but not too much, Jergens Hand Lotion into the very end of the fully extended condom trying desperately not to laugh out loud. Once this delicate task was completed, the condom was laid most lovingly on the floor of Ken's lunchbox; right on top of the wadded up wax paper that previously contained his sandwich. They quietly snapped both the left and right latch that secured the top of the black lunch box to the bottom section and Dad tip-toed back to the truck to place the lunchbox in exactly the same place where it had been moments ago.

The day was done and home the boys went. The routine in the Stannard house was very consistent. My mom would have the dining room all set for dinner by around 2:00 in the afternoon. Dad would arrive home somewhere between 4:30 and 5:00. He would come in the door into our kitchen and while handing over

[183]

his lunchbox to his wife, would give her a quick kiss and ask how her day was. They would chat it up for a bit and he would retire to the living room to read the daily paper while enjoy a cigarette, that would eventually kill him, before dinner was served. Today, however, was different.

Dad blasted through the door, handed over his lunchbox, gave his wife a whoosh of a kiss on the cheek, bolted by his sons like we were all middle kids, quick-stepped into the dining room where he took his seat at the head of the table. To his left was an end table. On the table sat a notepad and a rotary dial telephone. It was pretty obvious to the rest of the family that Dad was expecting a very important phone call; probably from the President. It was hard to imagine who else it could be that would have resulted in such odd behavior. We looked at Mom for some clues of which she had none. We all stood in the kitchen very perplexed.

Dad had not been home five minutes before the dial telephone began to ring. Oddly, he didn't answer the phone. Instead, he just let it ring. Now why on earth would he come dashing into the house seemingly expecting a very important phone call and then, when the phone does ring, just sit there like nothing was happening? He was a mystery.

The phone rang at least ten times before he extended his left hand to pick up the receiver.

At the Nichols house, things started nearly the same. Ken came home from work and while giving his wife a kiss and asking how her day was he, too handed over his lunchbox for his wife to clean up and prepare for tomorrow. Ken had kicked off his shoes and put on his slippers before retiring to his living room with his daily paper. Fortunately, he didn't smoke so he outlived his boss and best friend (for now anyway) by many years before succumbing to liver cancer.

The poor guy hadn't even gotten to the Funnies yet when there stood Jean in the entryway to their living room. She had something in her hand that remotely resembled a long, dead, giant, white worm. He never had a chance to get one word out.

"Ken Nichols, what is this?" his wife demanded. Was that a rolling pin in her other hand? Ken was at a slight disadvantage as the light was such that he really couldn't see just what the heck it was she was holding.

"I have no idea." he said with more than a little fear and anxiety noticeable his voice.

A major fight ensued with poor Ken totally bewildered as to why his now screaming wife was holding a spent condom and flailing it around as though it was she waving the white flag, when it was, in fact, Ken who was desperately trying to surrender. Jean would have none of it. She was just getting started when Ken offered his only defense.

"I have no idea what the hell is going on here, but why don't you call Jim. I was with him all day today working on a sink at the West Side Market."

Jean picked up the phone and dialed the Stannard residence. On or about the tenth ring, standing there fuming and fit to be tied, Jean heard the phone on the other end come out of its receiver.

"Hello" she said sternly. No doubt my father could detect the anger in her voice much like that old TV show, "Name That Tune", where the contestants would wager that they could name that tune in one, two or three notes. "This is Jean Nichols...."

Before she could get another word out she heard, "Hello. Oh, HI Jean. Say, how's Ken doing today? Generally when he doesn't come into work he'll call me to let me know." (As if Ken would ever miss a day of work....ever.)

[185]

We could hear the receiver on the other end of the line slam down from where we were in the kitchen. Well, this was most certainly strange enough. Ken had not come into work today and had not called. Both of these things were unthinkable. Dad hung up his receiver and proceeded to sit right there just staring at the phone as if he knew it would be ringing again soon. There was no attempt by Mom to start serving dinner, because to do so would be futile. She somehow knew that it would be cold long before Big Jim would take his eyes off the phone. He sat there staring.

Things were really starting to heat up at the Nichols house. Jean slammed down the phone and said, "You didn't go to work today???!!!"

SNAP. There goes the bee's penis.

Ken was now totally confused. He had no idea what was happening. It's hard to say what happened next, but it wasn't pretty. Ken somehow was able to grab the phone with one hand and dial Jim's number, while fending off blows from the rolling pin with the other hand.

Over the screaming Ken could hear the phone ring. Then ring again. Then again and again and again. "Pick up the fucking phone" he thought to himself.

At the Stannard house, we, Mom and the kids, stood in the doorway to the dining room and watched with amazement as, once again, the phone rang and rang and rang. Dad sat there just staring at it letting it ring away. Man, he was in such a yank to get a phone call and now that he's getting one, it seems like he couldn't care less.

Finally he picked up the receiver. "Hello."

"Listen, Jim, you've got to tell Jean what the hell is going on here. She's going to kill me." Ken pleaded.

"I can't hear you with all that noise in the background." Big Jim said. "I'll see you at work tomorrow." Click.

No one really knows what happened over the next 10 hours or so. Dad went to work the next day as did Ken. Dad came home that night, kissed Mom and asked how her day was. Ruffled the hair on his son's head, grabbed his paper and retired into the living room with a cigarette dangling in the corner of his mouth.

Somewhere out there is a bee with no penis. The queen lived happily ever after.

CHAPTER 16

Over the Falls

Perhaps the best way to prepare for Surviving a Recovery is to die. Well, OK, not really die, but come damn close to dying. I mean really close as in there is no fucking way you are going to live through where you are right now at this one moment in time.

By now you should just about be coming to grips with the concept of Surviving the Recovery. We've had bad times hit us and many, like you, lost everything. Now, as if a recession wasn't horrible enough, we are forced to survive a recovery from the Recession.

This might be compared to an injury during the Civil War. My ancestor was a man named Gen. George Jerrison Stannard. He was an interesting Vermont boy who joined the Civil War because it was the right thing to do at the time. As we like to say here in Vermont, "He done good".

He made it to General and oversaw the 2nd Vermont Brigade which defeated Gen. Pickett at Pickett's Charge in the Battle of Gettysburg. One could argue that had it not been for this Stannard we might all have a pronounced southern accent. Oh, the horror! Swapping an unintelligible Vermont accent for an unintelligible southern accent would be too much for any self-respecting Vermonter to bear.

I use George as an example to demonstrate how oftentimes a recovery can be slightly more traumatic than the initial event from which one is recovering. Case in point; Gen. Stannard was right handed. During one of his many battles, he was shot in his right arm with a .30 caliber musket ball. Although it's never happened to me, mind you, I would have to say that this had to hurt. By all due accounts, it did. But imagine the fear and loathing that had to be going through the good General's head about 2.5 seconds after that ball crashed into his arm.

George must've thought to himself, "Sumnabitch...now I have to go see the Doc."

Seeing a doctor because of a musket ball blowing your arm to pieces back then was a whole lot different than seeing a doctor today. His first thought had to have been, "They're probably going to have to cut this sucker off." By "this sucker", he meant his right arm. That was the solution to just about every gunshot wound back then; amputation.

So here George has this problem; a destroyed right arm (or in our case, a recession) and he's going to have to go in for treatment (or in our case, a bailout) and then recover; (in his case, suffer with gangrene for about two weeks before dying a horrible death; in our case, just trying to stay alive after losing everything.)

One could assume that George might have assumed that this one split-second moment when the ball hit the arm was the end for him. He would have his arm cut off. It would get infected and he would die what would feel like a long, slow, painful death and most likely never recover. Too bad you're not more like George.

Miraculously, George did not get gangrene and did not die. He went back home to Vermont to recover from his wounds. He went from a Brigadier General to a Major General with one arm. He served as a Door Keeper in Congress but, as it turned out, indoor jobs weren't his thing. He came back to his home in Vermont to face another problem. His house, like most houses, was outfitted for a right-handed person. Instead of sitting down and giving up, word has it that he made his own jigs and reconfigured all the door handles and hinges so that they would accommodate a left-handed person. I guess if you're used to getting your ass shot off in Civil War battles, the idea of retrofitting your home, using only one arm (the arm that you're not used to using), probably seems like a do-nothing challenge, don't you think? George lived to be an old man and by most accounts, was reasonably happy.

Therefore, if this one man could get shot in the hip (I left that wound out before), lose his right arm and not die from infection, come back and continue on as a Major General, move back to Vermont and retrofit a house with one hand (not his good one, either), then WHAT THE HELL ARE YOU COMPLAING ABOUT?

Sorry, I didn't mean to shout there, but geez, let's put this in some sort of perspective. Yes, we were crushed with a Recession and in your case, you lost everything you own. And now, we're confronted with Surviving a Recovery that appears to be only benefitting those who helped to create the Recession to begin with. It's not impossible to see how you might think that all is lost and that there's no hope however, how about we agree that going forward we should all be grateful that we don't have gangrene? Can we agree on that?

Good. Now, where were we? We were talking about dying; not really dying but damned well convinced that you're going to die and that's just about as bad as really dying; maybe worse.

The year is 1974. The month is April; early April. It was one of those fabulous Vermont days where if you stood in the warm sun it felt like heaven. It was about 55 to 60 degrees in the sun. After spending months freezing your ass off, that first warm, almost spring day feels damn near as good as sex. OK, it feels good. We'll leave it at that. It's that first day when you can comfortably sit in your lawn chair (provided you can find it under all of the snow that fell in March) with a piece of aluminum foil under your frighteningly white chin in hopes of going from wicked pale to just pale.

That's in the sunshine. In the shade it's about 28 degrees and what snow is around has the consistency of a glacier at the Arctic Circle. It was a great day for a hike. Not a long hike, mind you, but a hike nonetheless. Two of my best friends at the time, Helme and Jimmy, thought it would be a good idea to hike up to the waterfalls at Hager Brook in North Rupert. The brook runs under Rt. 30 right next to the historic sign alerting travelers to the fact that, at one time on this site, there sat a coin minting operation; Harmon's Mint. Yes, Vermont once minted its own currency. Some think the State went right to hell after we ceased doing so. Some today think we should go back to minting our own coins. At the rate the rest of the nation is going to hell, this may not be a bad idea. The coins were made of copper and probably left your fingers all green. It was about the only resource to be had other than wood and you do know about wooden nickels, I hope.

We parked our car in the pull off by the historic sign, which some think has been there longer than the actual minting plant, and started hiking up to the falls on the north side of the brook. The falls is not that far back in the woods, which is helpful as we decided that since it was such a glorious day, and we were doing something as life-threatening as walking over ice-crusted snow to a 60+ foot high waterfall also encased completely in ice, that we should smoke a joint or two before climbing our way to the top; as if our judgment warranted additional clouding.

In what felt like about a month or so, we reached the top of the falls. It was spectacular; breathtaking really. It was predominantly baby blue. The ice looked like molten candlewax that had been carefully dripped over boulders left behind after the glacier of millions of years ago ground down the mountain that was once as high as the Swiss Alps. It looked cold, but in an inviting sort of way.

Much to our surprise and good fortune, a storm from some time ago had blown down a tree that landed right across the brook about twenty feet back from where the brook headed over the cliff thus creating the magnificent waterfalls now frozen solid and glowing like London Blue Topaz.

Helme danced across the frozen, glistening log and to the other side of the brook much like a modern dancer. He was very graceful. Jimmy marched right along behind him. This looked easy enough as long as you weren't terrified of heights. I have been terrified of heights for as long as I could remember. Well, terrified might be a little strong, but if I have an option of staying on the floor or going up in the air, the floor looks like the better of the two choices.

"I got this" I thought to myself and placed my right foot on the log, then my left. "Best not to look over to the right where God knows how many gallons of water per minute are rushing over the cliff and adding another coat of ice to the already bulging, blue boulders way down there. Nope, eyes straight ahead; with the notable exception of looking down occasionally to make sure your feet are placed squarely on the log.

SPLAT! A firmly packed snowball hit me smack dead center in my stomach. I looked up and there was Helme straight ahead packing another snowball. Jimmy was 90 degrees off to my left.

"It's best we not fuck around here, boys" I said as Jimmy launched a snowball that just missed. I scurried across the log and was now on dry land. Well, not exactly dry. We were shaded by the pine trees that donned the area. The snow was covered with a frozen crust. If you stomped your foot you could break through it where, underneath, was nice wet, sticky snow; perfect for making snowballs.

I feverishly packed snow as snowballs went whizzing by. I'd throw at Jimmy. Helme would throw at me. I'd throw at Helme. Jimmy would throw at me. And on it went. We had a full-fledged snowball fight going on here and nothing else mattered. The beautiful sunny day had disappeared right along with the giant, blue boulders that looked like someone had poured thousands of gallons of power blue wax over them. The focus was 100% on flying snowballs.

The fight went on for what seemed like a few minutes longer than Pickett's Charge. The moment arrived when I had one snowball in my left hand and one in my right. My right arm was fully cocked and I was about to let one fly at Helme when I caught a glimpse of motion in the extreme corner of my left eye. I turned my head to the left to see a snowball flying at, or around, 50 mph and headed directly for my left eye.

Instinctively, I twisted to the right and ducked. The good news was that the screaming snowball missed my face by inches. The bad news was that in the process of wrenching my body to the right, I lost my balance, fell to the ground, and landed on my hands and knees. All would have been right with the world had not the centrifugal force of my spinning away from the screaming snowball not caused me to begin to slide towards the falls.

At first, I was stoned enough to rather appreciate the subtle sliding motion at a rate slightly slower than a painted turtle. That all came to an end however, when I started picking up speed and moving closer to the top of the waterfalls. The ground was very smooth; much like that of a skating rink and tilting downward towards the falls.

It felt like I was sliding in slow motion. The moment lasted forever. There came a time when I knew I was going over the falls. Repeated punching and kicking of the crust proved futile. I was sliding just fast enough so that I couldn't break through the crust and stop myself. This was not good. What were those guys going to tell my wife? "I told him not to smoke that joint." That would never fly.

Later Helme would say that he saw me disappear over the falls. Jimmy said that he could still see just the top of my butt, but that was it. What a way to go! At least I was unwittingly mooning the guy who threw the last snowball that would result in the end of my days here on earth. I was on the threshold of resigning myself to the fate that awaited me below.

At this point, I was well on my way to going over the falls. I couldn't stop my forward motion. I could see down into the falls. The boulders with their soft, magically blue molten coating would be what would break my fall; right along with every bone in my body. This was it. I was twenty-two years old. I had had a really good time thus far and was now ready to move on. I was almost excited about the prospects, primarily because there was little I could do about it. Shit, I might as well enjoy the ride. Look at the bright side. Those rocks were not only the hardest thing on the planet; they had the extra added benefit of being coated in ice. Any massive wounds sustained would be rendered numb instantly. This might have very well ended up being a perfect ending, notwithstanding the fact that it would be slightly premature. It was a most beautiful, sunny day with temperatures near 60 in the sun and I was stoned and sliding over the coolest frozen waterfall in Vermont where I would inevitably meet my doom.

I mean, this was damned near perfect. At least I didn't have my right arm shot off and had to stare down gangrene for a few weeks before baking to death from an enraged fever. No way. Instead, I was taking the cool way out by doing a face plant on blue-ice covered rocks. For years, maybe generations, people would say, "Oh yeah, he rocked" and then break into hysterical laughter!

Unfortunately, it was not meant to be (obviously because I'm here writing this, aren't I??). I was well past the point of no return. I had surrendered to my fate and trancended to the place where I was not only accepting the situation, but was starting to relish it. I'm sure that would have given way to absolute, sheer panic had I become airborne, but that would only have lasted about 1.2 seconds (or 10,000 eternities) before my head blew open from the impact of hitting the first boulder.

There was a little strip of rock outcropping about 4" long and about ¾" high on my right. I never even saw it. It just came in contact with the heel of my right hand. I felt it before I saw it. I was probably at or around a 90 degree angle and well on my way to a most certain death when I felt the pressure on my right palm.

I pushed. Oh baby, did I push. There was very likely about 10,000 PSI of pressure on this tiny piece of rock. I had the fleeting thought that maybe it might not hold, but pushed that out of my mind instantly. All I wanted to do right now was to stop moving forward. My elbow was pushed backwards beyond my back. My head was jutting out over the falls. I stopped. I could not believe that I had stopped.

I didn't linger on this act of good fortune very long, although it felt like I had entered the world of walking through molasses wearing lead boots. I pulled back my left arm and punched as hard as I could downward. My fist blasted through the crust. Whew, now I had both hands holding me from flying over the falls to a most certain, tragic, cold, but not without a lovely shade of blue, death.

Next went my right knee crashing through the crust, then my left. I was all set. All that I needed to do now was to wait about six weeks or so until all the snow melted away and I'd be fine. OK, that wasn't going to work. Let's look at "Plan B". Plan B consisted of removing my hand from the lifesaving outcropping of ledge and punching a hole with my right fist into the snow so that I could begin the process of backing up.

There are things we do in life that are easy. We go to the store and buy food. We go out to the movies. We hang out with friends and loved ones. Most of the time, living is pretty damned easy. Then there are the times when it's not. Removing one's palm from a tiny piece of rock outcropping that just saved one's life in order to punch another hole through the crust in order to back up six inches so that you don't fly over a frozen waterfall to a most certain cold and painful, (albeit a rather nice shade of blue), death, is one of those times.

Looking back over 62 years, I think one the hardest things I've ever done was to let up on that piece of rock. It was one of those all-or-nothing moments that don't come around all that often; one of life's little tests. It was one of those moments that you can actually feel your heart beating inside your chest. One of those moments when everything that was ever even remotely important to you (and some things that weren't all that important) fly through your mind in an instant. You see everyone you've ever known; everyone you've ever loved. It's like you're given one last chance to ponder on what was meaningful; if only for a second. It might just be the best, most important second of your entire life. It seems a shame that we get to enjoy that second for only a second and then we're outta here.

I got lucky. I was able to back my way out of my precarious situation. Once I got to the place where the ground leveled out, I decided it was safe to stand up. That was another big moment. I'm sure I crawled back way farther than I had to, but at this point, I was not taking any more chances, thank you very much. I got to my feet and looked around.

There stood Helme, straight ahead in the exact same position right where he was when I last saw him. I looked off to my left and there stood Jimmy as well. Both of these guys looked slightly more frozen than the lovely blue rocks that had captured my full attention only moments ago.

"Wow, that was a rush" I said. The two were speechless.

Finally Helme said, "I saw you go over."

"Yeah, I came back just for this" and plastered him with a snowball.

"OK, no more fucking around" he pronounced.

"Probably a good idea. We about done here?"

[198]

And with that we began our descent in total silence. We didn't say much until we got to the car. Once we were safely away from the place that was nearly my undoing I told them what it felt like. Then we never talked about it much.

Turned out the Recovery was just fine. It could've gone either way, but isn't that always the case?

CHAPTER 17

The Drone

Growing up in Vermont might be just like growing up anywhere else, but I doubt it. In 1950, there were only 378,000 thousand people living here. As of today, that number has just barely doubled. Maybe it's the climate or maybe it's the black flies, but for some reason, just not that many people want to live here. And for those who do choose to live here, we're OK with that. Vermont is not for everyone; and it shouldn't be.

It's a funny state. For reasons no one can seem to fathom, Vermont has fewer African Americans living here than any other state. There were more blacks here during the Civil War than were in the 1950s, which is understandable once you realize that Vermont sent more soldiers, per capita, to fight in the Civil War than any other state.

We tend to be a conservative state when it comes to spending a buck, but fairly liberal when it comes to dealing with Vermonters less fortunate. There is also one strict code by which most native Vermonters live: Mind your own goddamn business.

If your neighbor is gay, who gives a shit? If your gay neighbor comes to your house and suggests that you also be gay, then he's not minding his own goddamn business. Unless your neighbor is doing something that has a direct and demonstrably negative impact on you and the way you live, then it's none of your business.

Had our previous President, George Bush, been a Vermonter, as opposed to a Texan, he would never have invaded Iraq. His DNA would not have allowed it. He would've had to wait until Iraq was on our doorstep, at which time he could have easily justified reducing the place to rubble. Instead, he took an overt action and reduced the place to rubble. That would be considered bad form in Vermont.

Vermonters are a tolerant people, but don't think of them as pushovers. That would be a rather large mistake. I'm sure you're familiar with the boisterous slogan, "Don't Mess with Texas". Vermont has no such slogan, nor do Vermonters care that much about explaining their intent to the rest of the world. If, for whatever reason, you feel compelled to make the mistake of your life and mess with Vermont, don't expect to hear us chant out some fancy goofy slogan. You can, however, expect a return in kind to whatever it is you're offering. If you're nice and mind your own business, Vermont's the place for you. If you insist on telling people who they can love, or how they must live, well, let's just say that Vermont's not the place for you.

You can learn a lot from watching Vermonters. They're different. Think of it like going to the zoo and seeing if you can pick up some tips from the animals you see there. Here's an example: Tiger #1 is lying on the warm rocks peacefully minding his own business. Tiger #2, presumably from another part of the country, strolls on over to Tiger #1 and decides it might be fun to bat around Tiger #1's tail, which he proceeds to do.

Tiger #1 opens one eye; doesn't say anything, just opens one eye. The look is one of, "Best not fuck with my tail." Not knowing the nuances necessary for survival, Tiger #2 takes another, unnecessary, but perhaps personally satisfying swipe at Tiger #1's tail…WHAM!

It's all over in half a second. Tiger #2 has no idea what happened or what hit him. He's upside down, inside out, unconscious. Tiger #1 is right back where he had been a moment ago with both eyes closed resting peacefully.

Then there's the other Vermonter; the one that you're more apt to like, once you get to know him/her. This is the Vermonter that stops to see how you're doing after you've slid off a slippery, snowy road and are stuck up to your axles. This Vermonter will stand there for an unnervingly long time and just stare at you. Yes, you will be intimidated, but bear in mind that there's really only one thought flowing through his mind, which is, "Why do you have all-season tires on that rig?"

Of course, every Vermonter knows that it's bad form to actually ask questions like this, because we operate under the assumption that you have a fucking clue as to what you're doing. We think that way, primarily because we live that way. We don't make too many moves without knowing the outcome. It wastes a lot of time and energy; both considered to be number one and two on the list of high commodities. And this could be a major factor in what separates Vermonters from the rest of the species. We value money to the degree that we get that it's necessary to exist, but once you get beyond that, its relevance is diminished substantially when compared to time and energy.

Time is the great equalizer. Everyone, rich and/or poor, is born and given a certain amount of time to be here on the planet. How that time is invested directly determines how wealthy you will be when the time comes you're lying in a bed surrounded by loved ones wishing you well on your next journey. Fucking people out of their money so that you can amass a great fortune will reduce the number of people who will be with you at the end of your life.

When it gets right down to it it's pretty simple really. It's nothing more than prioritizing. You put what is most important to you first and then work your way down. If money is your top priority, then you'll end up with lots of things, but no friends. If friends are your top priority, you'll most likely end up with hardly any money at all, but would be considered by most as a very wealthy person.

Surviving the loss of money is nothing. Surviving the loss of friends; well that's something entirely different. It's much easier to make more money; less satisfying in the end, but much easier.

So back to growing up in Vermont of the '50s and early '60s; a time when things were very different from what you see today. There was no zoning or land use planning regulations. Those came into being because people found it hard to mind their own goddamn business. There were maybe one or two cops, because there was no real crime to speak of. The only dope around was who some considered to be the town drunk, Ferp Lake. Turned out old Ferp was smarter than just about everybody, but that's another story. Nobody was really doing anything bad, because it would be bad to do so. And if, by chance, you did bad, then you were expected to make amends. There was no real need for a whole lot of law enforcement back then.

Today you would be hard pressed to construct a huge metal ball in your front yard, get totally shitfaced and hop on a 1940s Indian motorcycle and drive around inside the ball.

Annie Jewel and her first husband, Ernie, owned the South Dorset General Store. It was nothing more than a one-pump gas station but they sold other provisions like milk, bread, eggs, and beer (the staples of life). They also sold penny candy, which was fortunate because hardly any kid in South Dorset ever had more than a penny. Should they find a way to do an odd job here and there and be awarded a few cents, it would be off to Annie's store for some candy and a soda.

There came a time when Ernie passed away. Then, there was a time when Annie ran the store by herself. Annie was great. She was very stern. She had to be. She ran a tiny store in a tiny town and had to scrape for every dime she got. Once you got past that scowl and crazy, messy blonde hair that went every which way and that, she could be awfully nice. She was really no different than any other Vermonter. If you treated her right, she was your friend. If you crossed her....well, let's just stop right there. Nobody crossed Annie Jewel. Period.

After an acceptable period of time for mourning the loss of Ernie, Annie remarried. She married Ray Wright. To this day, I don't know anything about Ray's past; his family; nothing. He was an interesting character. To say he was a little grungy would be like saying Marilyn Monroe was slightly sexy. He always seemed just a little too dirty, which was a mystery because he never seemed to do a lot of work. Maybe he got greasy from working on his motorcycles. It's hard to say.

He would clean his hands up now and then when he would reach down behind the counter next to the chair where he would sit when he would entice you into playing a game of checkers, and pull out his violin. Running a one-pump gas station in a very small town in a very quiet time could get on your nerves. To steady his nerves, Ray drank a lot of beer. It seemed to work pretty well, too because he never really got too excited. There would be a slew of South Dorset ne'r-do-wells hanging around not amounting to much when suddenly out would come the violin. I never learned who taught Ray how to play or if he just figured it out on his own, but looking back, he was a pretty good fiddle player; notwithstanding the somewhat negative impact of a six-pack might have on the final product of his playing.

He'd be fiddling away while Annie was busting her butt stocking shelves and pumping gas for those who stopped by. After a while, he'd put the fiddle aside and asked if anyone wanted to play a game of checkers. This was a sore subject for just about every kid in town. I don't recall anyone ever beating Ray in a game of checkers. One of us would take the challenge (or bait) and sit in the rickety old chair that was directly across from Ray. You had to look directly at the creases and crevices that made up his scraggy face. The bloodshot eyes alone would cause any kid to lose their concentration.

Mercifully, a game of checkers with Ray never lasted very long. He'd whoop your ass in no time. "Care for another game?" he'd cheerfully ask while taking a pull from a brown paper bag that we all knew contained a beer from the cooler that was off to the left. Those of us with determination and undying spirit would accept the challenge only to be roundly defeated in minutes.

There was no real humiliation in getting beat by Ray, because everyone got beaten by Ray. Playing checkers with Ray Wright was the great equalizer. The side of Ray's road was littered with kids he had defeated over the years.

Now I can hear you asking, "Why would you go back to this store almost every day just to get your sorry ass whooped in checkers, after spending every penny you had on buying his candy and soda pops?"

Of course, you would have to ask, because you don't have a firm grip on punishment and reward. After Ray beat every kid crazy enough to accept his challenge and left the room silent with kids with moping faces all, once again, staring at the floor in shame, Ray would smile this huge smile exposing some of the nastiest teeth you've ever seen and ask, "Anyone want to watch me ride?"

We were frozen in anticipation of what be about to happen. You could hear a fly fart over in the pond across the street created by the old mill dam long since done operating. Well, yeah, of course we wanted to see Ray ride because it was an opportunity to see if this man who beat us every day at checkers would finally kill himself doing a most insane stunt when he was way more than half in the bag.

Watching Ray get out of the rickety old chair that was held together with a crisscross of wires that seemed to work, lord knows how, was almost as much fun as watching him ride. He'd get up and put one hand on the counter, presumably to steady himself and stop the room from spinning. There were times when he would take that first step left towards the door which was on the north side of the building then back up and stagger off to the right. Lucky for him, the ice cream freezer was right there for him to place his right hand on. He'd stop and assess the situation before taking another courageous step.

No kid would dare speak, but we all seemed to have a telepathy thing going on; sort of like Sookie Stackhouse in True Blood. We would all be thinking, "How can this guy, who can barely even walk, expect to get on a 1940s Indian motorcycle and ride in the huge metal drone that he had spent all spring constructing?"

The drone went up one piece at a time. First, the bottom platform was pieced together offering little, if any, clue as to what was about to be created. Then the lower, curved, mesh panels were bolted to the bottom platform. One of these panels contained a door that you had to remember to lock once inside the drone and riding or else you'd have the pothole from hell.

More curved panels were hoisted into place and securely (or hopefully securely) bolted together. The few people around back then that had cars would stop as they drove on their way into Manchester for provisions and gawk at the alien sphere that was coming to life with each passing day. Even when it was completed, no one had a clue as to what it was. It must've been good for business, because people would stop every day and ask Ray what he was building. I don't ever recall him responding to any question ever, so I doubt anyone left with an adequate answer.

The day finally came when the drone was completed. Like I said, most people still didn't know what the hell it was. That is until the day when Ray hopped on his 1940s Indian motorcycle and started to ride.

Just getting on the bike was something to watch. Sometimes he'd actually tip it over and crash to the ground. I'm sure you can all appreciate the fact that it's easier to be in motion than stationary when it comes to sitting on a bike. We were very understanding and appreciative of the fact that he probably had at least a quart of beer in him (he never drank small cans or bottles of beer. He only drank quarts of beer and seemed to have a quart going constantly).

Ray drove the old, dependable bike up the ramp and into the drone. He didn't bother to dismount to secure the door, thank God, because who knows what would have happened had he done so. Dumping the bike while standing still was always embarrassing; not that Ray ever seemed to give a shit if he found himself in an embarrassing situation (more on that later). He hit the throttle and off he went.

At first, he just went around in a circle a few feet above the bottom platform. A half a dozen kids had their eyes glued to Ray thinking for sure that there was no way he was going to make it out of this steel cage alive. It's not every day that you get to watch someone intentionally kill themselves on a vintage bike. Even though we had no real appreciation of its value, we were very concerned for the bike. I should note that he also had an ancient Harley Davidson that he would use. No one ever asked why he would choose one bike of the other, because we knew no answer would be forthcoming.

Ray pulled back on the throttle of the ancient Indian and guided the bike further up the rounded surface. By now some of us had climbed up the stairs on the outside of the drone to a spectator's platform that would allow one to look down into the drone. We were so close that we could see Ray's bloodshot eyes staring straight ahead. The level of concentration and focus necessary to pull this stunt off while sober was not inconsequential. Pulling this off while dancing with a blood alcohol content of somewhere over 2.0 was, to say the least, masterful. It taught us early on that drinking while driving was not a good thing to do unless you were doing so inside a steel ball 25' high barely bolted together.

The drone would shake every time Ray passed by the upper viewing stand. Although we were terrified that the entire steel ball would explode and we'd all fall to a most certain death, no one would ever dare move to leave the platform. Are you kidding me? This was the absolute best view ever to watch someone totally destroy themselves on a vintage Indian motorcycle. There was no way anyone was moving an inch. Plus, and I can admit this now some 50+ years later, we were scared shitless, and when one is scared shitless, there will be no moving.

Round and round Ray went. It was hard to tell exactly how fast he was going but it was enough to defy gravity and that was all that mattered. How the hell was he ever going to come down from riding right near the very top of the drone? Backing off the gas too much would result in certain death. He would go crashing down to the bottom of the steel sphere and that would be the end of him. Oh, the poor bike!

Ray slowly backed off the gas and expertly guided the bike back down to the platform. He removed his helmet and looked up to see a crowd of applauding 10 year olds who were nothing short of astonished to have witnessed a thoroughly intoxicated and albeit somewhat grimy, crinkly faced old man defy gravity. It was absolutely THE most spectacular thing anyone had ever witnessed in South Dorset; hell, in all of Dorset for that matter.

Ray had survived the impossible. We all left the platform to greet Ray as he opened the cage door and exited on his bike, which he stored in the shed next to the store. The whole thing was magnificent, but what was really interesting was that when it was all over, nobody ever said a word about it. If you asked Ray how the hell he stayed up on the very top of the drone without crashing to the bottom, he'd just look at you. It was clear no answer was forthcoming, again. Sometimes one of us would ask a question only to be greeted by silence accompanied with a slight grin.

"Anyone want to play a game of checkers?"

"Sure." I said. I'm pretty sure I can beat you this time, Ray. Can I have a soda, though?"

I got my ass kicked and didn't mind a bit. There were some incredible times to be had in that little one-pump gas station. I guess you had to be a kid and had to be there to appreciate them. Looking back it had to be a pretty novel thing to have a motorcycle drone set up in your town's one-pump gas station. We thought it was pretty darned cool but like everything else in life, after a while it just became commonplace. Yeah, we'd walk a mile down to the store with a pocket full of pennies and yeah we'd buy some candy and sodas and yeah, we'd get our asses kicked in checkers and then treated to a little fiddle music and yeah, then we'd go outside and watch Ray ride around in circles in his drone. What's the big deal? Doesn't everybody have a life like this?

Before Ray died, he did present me with my first introduction to sex. Now, before you get all twisted up here, let me qualify that statement by saying that Ray was no pervert, but for reasons that no one on this earth could ever explain, women appeared to be attracted to Ray. It must've had something to do with his daredevil image. Who knows?

Anyway, I was walking in the door to the store one day, just like any other day, and there was Ray and some woman that I recognized from Dorset. They both looked very surprised when I walked in which I thought was an odd reaction inasmuch as the store was open for business. Ray had the lady from Dorset right up on the ice cream freezer. Her dress was hiked up and his pants were down slightly lower than normal. Ray invented the droopy, show some butt crack, image long before the kids of today picked it up.

I was a little too young to get what the heck was going on. I recall that the first thought that came into my mind was, "Jeez, that freezer has got to be some cold on her bare butt!" My next thought, once I realized what was happening was, "I sure do hope that Annie doesn't come walking in right about now because there will be two dead people in the room; three if she doesn't want any witnesses."

My final thought was that it would be a long time before I'd get ice cream out of that freezer. I was OK with sticking with candy and soda pop from the cooler and maybe getting my ass whooped in a game of checkers.

After that, life just went on. Ray never offered an explanation and if you think I was ever going to ask a question, you'd have another thing coming. Some things are best left unanswered; kind of like, "How the hell do you keep that bike from falling?"

You can appreciate how Surviving a Recovery may not be as easy as one might think.

CHAPTER 18

Black Sheets

As I've stated ad nauseam here, things are getting better. We are on the Yellow Brick Road of Recovery in these here United States of America. Things are looking up and we'd be a hell of a lot further on down the road if you'd work just a little harder on your positive attitude.

It's been proven time and time again (by me, anyway) that if you mope around saying things are for shit, then things are for shit. But, if you take a more positive approach and say, for instance, "Well, things are for shit, but they ain't as bad as they could be", then you're already making headway. You're halfway home to the land of prosperity just by thinking you might get there.

Let me give you an example. Almost every day we read about some crazy bastard strapping explosives to him or herself and blowing themselves, and everything around them, to smithereens. Now, there has to be a damned sight more positive thinking going into that one act than anything you've got going on, don't you think? I mean, someone has got to convince that person that things are really, truly looking up for them to blow themselves to bits.

So, you can see that power of positive thinking really does work. I'm hoping that we don't have to spend a lot of time here trying to convince you that if you just take a few small steps you're going to a place with 72 virgins. However, if that's what it takes to get your head out of your ass and set you straight, then by God, do we have a corral full of virgins just waiting for you.

Now, don't you feel better? You're ready to go and dive head first into that stream that will take you right on down to ocean of Recovery. Things are going to be just fine. OK, so you're broke and you have zero prospects or any hope of ever regaining the fortune you lost. Shit, cheer up. No one's asking you to blow yourself up in some abstract hope of coming into, uh, bad choice of words here, hooking up with 72 virgins. Of course, it'd just be your luck that the 72 virgins would all be the nuns at the Catholic school you attended, and they are all probably armed with AK-47's but hey, at least they're virgins, right! Look on the bright side.

There's no way you can ever hope to survive the Recovery if your head's not in the game. There is always a dark side and there is always a bright side. Maybe I can explain this a little more clearly for you.

It would be around 1963. It was winter and it was a corker. We had snow on top of more snow and we had just got another dumping of the white stuff. This could only mean two things. First, the roads weren't going to be plowed for a day or two. Second, there'd be no school.

Next, there wasn't much else to do but go sliding. There was a decent hill behind my grandparent's place on Rt. 30, which conveniently was right across the street from our house. Since there was no school, the neighborhood kids of South Dorset congregated behind John and Lucy's house (my grandparents) and proceeded to drag their device of choice up the hill. Some kids had old, beat and dented flying saucers. The wealthier kids (not that there were any in South Dorset) had a toboggan or maybe a Flexible Flyer sled. The Flexible Flyers were, for the most part, pretty useless in deep snow. They performed much better on icy roads, such as Morse Hill Road as it's known today. In 1963 it was still called Nigger Hill. I was always mystified by this title as there was not a black person anywhere in southern Vermont that I could see. Years later I would learn from my Uncle Dick Stannard that this road got its name because it was where the very poor Irish lived who came here during the great potato famine in Ireland. Apparently, poor Irish were in the same category as poor blacks. Who knew? It wasn't until sometime later that the Town became somewhat more politically correct and renamed the road. It was bound to happen eventually and it's a good thing, too. It'd be really hard to explain this road with its previous name to my grandkids; both of whom are of mixed race. When they get older, I'll have them read this book.

Anyway, this was a time when, if we got enough snow, you could actually sled down Morse Hill Road. It would be considered about the dumbest thing you could do as the road comes to a "T" intersection with Rt. 30. Back then, there wasn't a whole heck of a lot of traffic on Rt. 30; especially on days when we'd have a big storm. It was nothing like the summertime when my older brother, Jim, came flying down this same road on a one-speed bike with no brakes. He flew out into Rt. 30 right in front of an on-coming car. He just missed the car. That was the good news. He did, however, slam into the cable that went from post to post and served as a guardrail and flew into the yard of the people who lived at the base of the hill. How he didn't break a bone was one of those unsolved mysteries.

But, back to sledding. A line of kids looking like ants in search of food hiked up the hill and slid back down over and over again. Of course, with each new passing, the trail got packed harder and harder. We had to be careful because there was a barbed wire fence way down at the bottom which was designed to keep you from crashing into the stone wall. This was definitely not an OSHA approved trail; not that there was any such thing as OSHA then.

We had a great day of sledding. Towards the end of the day, when we're all pretty beat, my father showed up to see what we were all up to. He admired the trail we had blazed and how close we had come to the fence without actually ripping our faces off. You could see the look of pride on his face.

"Do you kids know the one thing better than sledding?" he asked.

Uh, well, there is nothing better than sledding so a group of over a dozen kids just stood there slack-jawed and speechless.

Not one for caring much about waiting for answer to a question that he already has the answer for he said, "Sledding at night."

Say what? Great idea but in the dark we were certain to run into the fence and God knows what else.

"How are we going to be able to go sledding in the dark, Dad? We won't be able to see anything!"

"I have an idea." he said and off he went down to the barn. He was gone for a while and when his head popped out of the door he hollered, "I could use a little help here."

Kids went running down the snowy field falling ass over tobacco box, getting up and racing each other towards the barn. It turned out the barn was full of old, discarded tires from the various trucks used at the plumbing company my grandfather owned.

"Here, you kids grab a tire and take them up to the trail you've made. Put one on one side and one on the other. Stagger them one in front of the other. Start at the top and space them evenly so you have at least one left for the bottom. You'll want that bottom one up about 30 feet or so from the fence so you'll know when to stop." Dad was always thinking about our safety.

All in all, we must've had close to a dozen or fifteen tires staggered down the trail. "Now, go home and have some dinner and plan to be back here by 7:00 p.m." he instructed. Off we went.

When we got home, I couldn't wait to tell my mom what was going to happen after dinner.

"Are you sure this is a good idea, Jim?" Mom asked skeptically. As a rule, she played the role of wet blanket on just about all of Dad's great ideas. My brother and I were holding our collective breaths praying that he would not rethink his plan.

"Thyra, you worry too much."

[217]

Atta boy, Dad!! We gobbled down dinner and put back on our wet snow pants. I had an old black and red wool hunting jacket that weighed a ton dry. It was still wet from the afternoon's sledding so it had to weigh at least two tons now. I couldn't care less that it was wet.

The neighborhood ne'r-do-wells showed up right on schedule. Unbeknownst to us, my father had gone back to the trail when no one was there and soaked the tires in kerosene. As we were all getting ready to fumble our way through the dark and try to find the trail, Dad hollered out, "Wait a minute."

First, the bottom tire erupted in flames. In the yellow light, we could see Big Jim, as he was known, dashing up the hill with a soldering torch in his hand. He paused to ignite the next tire, and then took off towards the next tire, and so on.

"Come on, you kids going sledding or are you just going to stand there all night?"

That was about all the coaxing we needed. A herd of kids stampeded their way to the top of the hill. By the time we arrived at the top, my father had lit up all of the tires. Now, if you've never set a discarded rubber tire on fire, then you have no idea just how hot they burn. Aside from turning into a blaze that is virtually impossible to extinguish, they have the extra added benefit of becoming very, very gooey; along with being very flammable. It didn't take much to appreciate my mother's skepticism on this "good idea".

Kids were flying down the previously packed trail that had now frozen over pretty well and was very fast. In no time, we would fly down the hill and nearly crash into the barbed wire designed to save us from the certain death of crashing into the stonewall.

Flames of four and five feet high were licking the jet black sky. Billows of black smoke poured off each tire and hung in the frigid air. Sure, years later we would learn that burning rubber was about THE most toxic thing in the universe, but on this cold winter's night, these burning tires were about the coolest thing that had ever happened in South Dorset.

Kids were sliding and laughing and laughing and sliding. My dad sat at the top of the hill and just watched. He looked like the conductor of a burning orchestra. At one point, I dashed down the hill with my extremely dented saucer spinning out of control. I lost it and rolled right over the top of one of the gooey, burning tires. Molten, burning rubber stuck to my coat.

I was freaking out when I heard my father yell out, rather nonchalantly considering the severity of the situation, "Just roll around in the snow. That'll put the fire out."

I always did appreciate how calm he would be in the face of adversity. I guess, since I was the middle child, perhaps I was more expendable; who knows? I was rolling back and forth like a madman and sure enough I was able to extinguish the flames. My worn black and red wool coat was now more black than red. It was covered with once-burning rubber goo that had adhered to it. At least the fire was out. I jumped back on the saucer and off I went down to see if I could reach the barbed wire designed to save me from the certain death of hitting the stonewall.

All great evenings must come to an end and this night was no different. Every kid in South Dorset who was sliding down the hill behind my grandparent's house in the glow of burning tires retired to their respective homes and I guarantee, slept like newborns. We were all exhausted, wet, smelled of burnt tires, and had never had more fun in our lives.

The next morning, the beige, Bell Telephone that resided on the antique end table that sat to the left of my dad's place at the head of the table began to ring. With the possible exception of the time Ken Nichols' wife, Jean, had called the house, Dad always answered the phone after the first ring. The idea of keeping a plumbing customer waiting was unacceptable. He picked up the receiver to hear the voice of Barbara Sheldon.

Harry and Barbara Sheldon lived at the foot of Morse Hill Road. Harry was one of the handiest men around and worked for the wealthier people of Dorset (and some not so wealthy) plowing driveways, taking down a tree or two, doing carpentry work and anything else that was required of him that he felt competent to do.

Barbara stayed home and raised their children. Many years later, they would open up a little farm stand where they would sell a few items like eggs, milk, and other staples. Their biggest items were Christmas trees. Harry had worked a deal with a landowner to allow him to grow Balsams. He tended to them all year long and would harvest the ones that were ready right around November. He sold a lot of trees. Harry spent a lifetime doing what most Vermonters do, which is to try to figure out how to live a lifetime.

It's hard for most people to come to grips with the idea that you may just be able to get through life without having a job. By that I mean one job. Most people get up in the morning and go to work at the same job for 30 years. There was a time when you could do that and retire at the end with a decent pension.   Companies have long since figured out a way to no longer offer pensions and instead setting employees up with 401-Ks that are managed by some money guy who charges plenty of hidden fees. By the time you're done, most of that money you socked away you socked away for the money guy. It's a pretty slick deal, really and if Vermonters had been raised to parents who taught them how to bilk people out of money then it would stand to reason that this idea would have come from a Vermonter. Unfortunately, most Vermonters were born to parents who put great emphasis on the difference between right and wrong. This upbringing has really held many Vermonters back. It's such a shame.

In lieu of having "A" job, Vermonters learned generations ago that in order to survive, you need to have the ability to do many jobs. The more you know and can do the better the chances of someone needing what you know and can do. I know what you're thinking.

You're sitting out there saying to yourself, "Yeah, but damn, that means you've got to hustle to find enough work to keep you going all the time. With a job, you don't have to worry about that. You just get up in the morning, go to your job, work eight hours, and go home. That job will be there tomorrow and you never have to worry about how and when you're going to make your next dollar."

Well there, Sherlock, how's that working out for you today? You spend twenty-nine years at one job and you're just about to retire when one day you go into work and you're informed that the stable company you've worked for forever is shutting down and moving to China. Now what? You're only trained to do one thing; put widget "A" into compartment "B". It's been fine for a long time and you've done OK with it but you're not quite ready to retire. You have no other real skills. You're forced into tapping that 401-K, which your money guy informs you will incur more fees for drawing out your own money prematurely.

A couple of things here. Should someone ever tell a Vermonter that they can't have their own money back, a war will ensue. This is why most Vermonters hide their money in a weatherproof container (they've come a long ways since the days of tin cans) and bury it in their backyard. Vermonter's are slightly more cautious than say, you. Unlike you, they (Vermonters) tend not to live too extravagantly, and two, they tend to live longer. You lived pretty high on the ol' hog and now are broke. In all likelihood, it'll be a miracle if you live long enough to finish this book. Most Vermonters will still be around to read my next book, if they cared to which, in all likelihood, they wouldn't. They already know all this stuff.

So who's better off in the end? The guy who did the same thing year in and year out only to get screwed at the end of his life, or the guy who got screwed almost every day and figured out a way around getting screwed so that he could survive the screwings?

I guess it's a matter of personal preference. Kind of like figuring out how to cook the Thanksgiving Day turkey. Some folks do it the traditional way by putting the bird in an oven and cooking it until it's perfectly done. Others toss it into a deep fryer in their garage to see if the can, A: get the turkey done in time for the football game, and B: burn down the garage and collect on their insurance. Ask yourself just who is having the more exciting Thanksgiving dinner.

The phone rang only once. "Oh Hi Barbara, how are yo….."

"You want to know how I am. I'm mad as hell, that's how I am!"

"I see, well now just what is the proble……"

"You know damn well what the problem is and don't say you don't."

It was not every day that we would get to witness my father knocked off center, but today was one of those days.

"I'm not quite following you here, Barbar….."

"You got all the kids to go sledding up behind John and Lucy's house last night."

"Well, yes that's true and the kids did seem to have a good time. Is that a proble…"

"Yes, it's a PROBLEM. I hung my sheets out to dry on the clothes line last night. When I went out to get them this morning they were clean and white on the south side. The north side was darn near black as coal. I couldn't imagine for the life of me how those sheets got all black until I heard you were burning tires to light up the field."

Uh oh.

"Like I said, Barb, the kids just had the best time. Tell you what you do. Go down to the store today and buy all new sheets, and anything that might have been on the line last night, and tell me how much it comes to."

"Oh, OK. I can do that. Oh, that'll be fine. You know some of those sheets were getting along; I may not have to replace ALL of them."

"You go right ahead and replace all of them. Everything else OK? How's Harry doing?"

"Harry's fine. He's over here laughing his fool head off."

"Tell him I said 'HI'. Anything else?"

"You know, you really shouldn't be burning tires in the middle of the night. Those kids might've killed themselves."

"Yeah, they might've, but it did look like they were having a pretty good time. Get me the bill for the sheets."

Perhaps the reason we had a recession in the first place was because no one would ever 'fess up. There seems to be a lack of wanting to take responsibility for one's actions. People screw up every day. That's not news but over time, we seemed to have morphed from a people that once stood up and said, "Yeah, I fucked up. Now what do I have to do to make it right?" to a people that deny culpability.

Granted, sometimes the debt owed is more than a couple of sets of sheets, but the philosophy is the same. You break it; you own it. Is that so hard?

[223]

CHAPTER 19

A Most Interesting Fishing Expedition

Obviously a great deal of preparation is necessary if one is hoping to have a muskrat's whisker of a chance to Survive the Recovery. We are going to go out on a limb here and speculate that you haven't done shit yet. Are we right?

You've been lying around in your discarded appliance box thinking to yourself, "Dang, this Recession's gonna last forever."

It's clear you've never heard of a guy named George Harrison. He was a member of a little rock band back in the '60s. After that band broke up, he did some work on his own. He was a survivor. He wrote a song called, "All Things Must Pass". It's also the title of an album he did.

He was right, too. All things do pass and the Recession that you thought was going to go on forever is now in our rear view mirror (although we might assume that wreck that you're driving might not have a rear view mirror) and now we are comfortably in the time of Recovery. You must be able to feel it, no? Probably because you're numb. Don't worry. You'll thaw out…just like we did.

There is only thing worse than fishing for four hours and only catching one fish and that is being so cold and numb that you're dumb enough to throw that one fish back into the lake. From the fish's perspective, it's great. He goes through a bit of a bad spell (by biting onto a treble hook and having it secure him to a line of certain peril) and gets hauled out of his comfort zone. Like you, he flops around aimlessly somehow thinking that all the flipping and flopping will have positive results (it won't). At some point, reality sinks in and the fish stops flopping and acquiesces to certain doom. This is about where you are in your thinking. You've entered the "cease flopping" stage. Your defeatist mind is kicking in and all you can think of now is just how hot that frying pan is going to be.

Your problem is that you need to have more of a positive attitude.

In the late fall of 2013, I found myself in my boat with two other guys. One was a man named Ed Aigletinger (he goes by Ed, thankfully) and the other was Jonathan Goldsmith; an actor who plays The Most Interesting Man in the World in the Dos Equis beer commercial. "How the hell did HE end up in your boat?" you ask. Just sit tight, would you?

The day before we had planned to go fishing in a lovely bass lake the weather was pretty fine. It was about 60 degrees and sunny. It was a near perfect fall day and any day is a near perfect day to go fishing. The three of us were very excited about the planned fishing expedition for the following day.

The weather forecast for the following day didn't look nearly as encouraging, but that was OK because notwithstanding today, when they said it was going to be sunny and 60 degrees, they are hardly ever right. Who would ever have guessed that the weather would be right two days in a row?

The forecast called for a light shower in the morning and cloudy the rest of the day. Temperatures would be around 50 degrees. OK, not so bad. This is why they invented Gore-Tex. Having once fished from a blowup rubber raft in 30 degree temperatures, hell, this would feel like surfcasting in the Bahamas (not that I've ever done that). With my boat secured to the back of my truck, I drove to The Most Interesting Man in the World's home where he and Ed were waiting. Waiting might not be the right word inasmuch as they weren't ready to roll so some time was spent farting around. If you fish you know you must allocate plenty of time; i.e. hours, farting around getting ready to fish verses actually fishing. This process is enhanced significantly if it's raining and the temperature is 50 degrees.

"You ready?"

"Just about."

Three hours later we're in the truck on our way to a lake where we've never fished. No, you're not going get the name of the lake. Those who fish are pretty closed mouthed about talking about where they fish...or about anything else for that matter (see conversation above).

Unfortunately, this lovely lake that we'd never fished before is a mountain lake. And not just any mountain lake, but a mountain lake that is way the fuck up on the top of a mountain. Did I mention it was lovely? Or, perhaps it would be more accurate to say that it had the potential to be lovely were it not for the drizzling rain that stubbornly kept spilling out of the sky.

Nearly an hour's drive later (and about $37.37 worth of gas), we arrive at our destination. I did mention that this was a mountain lake, right? One might think that after living in Vermont for eight generations that one might recall that the air is always slightly cooler in the mountains than in the valleys. When you're on your way to a fishing expedition, all you can think about is fish. The weather is incidental. That's why they invented Gore-Tex.

Fortunately, located in the top of my dashboard of my huge truck is a control panel that shows you everything except CNN News. We were able to watch the temperature descend as we ascended the mountain. By the time we got to what some might have construed to be a boat launch (the boulders all over the place served to disguise the launch nearly perfectly), the temperature had fallen to about 40 degrees. That was the good news. The bad news was that the drizzling rain that prompted the need for only intermittent wipers had now increased to a pretty steady rain; not a downpour, mind you, but just a nice steady rain. It was saving up for the downpour.

There's something else you should know about mountain lakes in the not-yet-but-soon-to-be-pouring-rain which is that those clouds that you see that hide the mountain when you look up from the valley transform into dense fog once you arrive at the top of the mountain. The visibility on this presumably lovely lake was maybe a quarter mile. Inasmuch as the lake is fifteen miles long, you might think that we would have been intimidated to go out in a boat with limited visibility, not unlike Ray Charles crossing the Los Angeles Freeway. No way. This was a fishing expedition and much like the fishing expedition initiated by Rep. Darrell Issa on the incident at Benghazi, we would not be deterred no matter what.

You know that you're in for a great day of fishing when you watch the man who plays The Most Interesting Man in the World struggle to get his pipe lit. There was never any question that this pipe would be lit at some point; it was just a matter of time. My cigar, on the other hand, was a different story. I stood a better chance of lighting a freshly laid dog turd than getting, and keeping, this sucker lit. One would expect nothing less from The Most Interesting Man in the World, other than dogged determination. Jonathan was born in the Bronx and this fucking pipe was going to be lit and he was not taking no for an answer. It was hard not to believe that with this kind of focus and resolve that the fish would be no contest.

The fish turned out to be more of a struggle than the pipe and/or the cigar. After about thirty minutes, we discovered that Gore-Tex, although a very catchy name, does little to keep one dry. Water is, after all, water and has the uncanny ability to find its way to just about anywhere it damned well pleases. It found its way everywhere. Seasoned fishermen understand this and fully expect to be soaked when it's raining. They have no problem suffering the consequences, or for that matter, just plain suffering. Getting soaked to the bone in 40 degree not-yet-but-soon-to-be-pouring rain just adds to the ambiance.

With pipes and cigars almost, but not quite, lit it was time to put a line in the water. Ed is a boat captain by trade and has an aversion to sitting down while fishing. Ed might just be The

Most Tough Man in the World, because he never sat down in the four-plus hours that we were out on that lake getting soaked to the bone and not catching a goddamn thing.

At one point, I took pity on him and offered him my backup pair of gloves. "I can't fish with gloves." was his reply. I didn't quite understand what fishing had to do with anything as we had not had so much as a nibble in over an hour.

The day progressed. The rain fell harder and then had the decency to back off a little before really dumping on us. Throughout it all, Ed never sat down. He only sat down when we moved the boat from one place that had no fish to another place that had less fish. He seemed perfectly happy being soaked to the bone, with frozen fingers, not catching anything. The Most Interesting Man in the World and I were perfectly happy watching this stoic figure, Ed, who could very well be The Most Tough Man in the World, standing like a frozen statue just waiting for that big one to bite onto his lure.

In what can only be described as an extraordinary event, suddenly Ed's pole bent way over. The Most Interesting Man in the World and I were stunned. We weren't sure just what to do. We were too cold and wet to actually move. Our respective pipe and cigar had gone out long ago and neither of us had it in us to take another run at lighting them. The last thing we had expected after all this time was that anyone would actually catch a fish. Man, leave it to a guy from Florida to ruin a good day of sitting in a perfectly nice boat, getting drenched and near freezing to death.

Once it appeared for real that Ed was about to reel in a fish, we started scurrying around for things like a net. The Most Interesting Man in the World retrieved the net from somewhere and with speed unlike anything I've ever witnessed, darted to the bow of the boat, fully extinguished pipe securely latched between his teeth, and was immediately on the ready to net whatever was on the end of Ed's line.

[230]

Now the four pound bass that had made the fatal decision to chomp onto Ed's lure simply had to be the absolute dumbest fish on the planet. I mean, that day there were probably no fewer than a million bass in this lake; hell maybe ten million for all I know, and each and every one of them were laying around equally freezing to death saying to each other, "Uh, you wanna bite that lure over there?" while the bass next to him replied "What are you, fucking nuts?"

All we could think was that it had to be some sort of dare. Bass number one looking over at bass number two and saying something like "You don't have a stiff dorsal fin if you don't bite on to that lure over there." and sure enough, that dumb bastard fish number two took the dare. Whatever it was that caused this one, and only one fish in a lake 15 miles long and God knows how wide to decide to bite onto Ed's lure, I doubt we'll ever know.

After putting up a good fight, The Most Interesting Man in the World scooped that big sucker out of the lake and into the boat. With hands slightly steadier than those of a brain surgeon, he whipped out a pair of forceps and with great skill and dexterity removed the hook from the lip of the bass. The bass didn't seem to mind a bit. Frankly, I think the bass was amazed at finally getting to meet up close and in person the man who plays The Most Interesting Man in the World. He sure was about to have a great human story to bring back to all his fish friends.

"I guess we should throw him back." Ed said.

"Yeah, probably." said The Most Interesting Man in the World.

Before I had a chance to weigh in with, "Are you fucking kidding me? This is the only fish we've caught all day long and I'm starving." we heard ka-splash. That big, beautiful bass darted down to the bottom never to been seen again.

"Don't worry" said The Most Interesting Man in the World. "There're more where he came from." It was hard not to admire his positive attitude; something lacking in the world today.

Well, maybe if we had brought along a few sticks of dynamite we might have been able to raise one or two more to the surface, but it was clear that our lures weren't going to do the trick. We suffered through more rain and declining temperatures for about another half an hour before finally calling it quits.

I started the motor and off we went zooming into the fog hoping that maybe we might find the place where we launched the boat. Since I'm here writing this, it should be apparent that we did find the spot and were able to get the boat out of the water and onto the trailer. The three of us piled into the truck and I immediately turned the heat to full blast. We had about a 45 minute ride ahead of us and I was most sincerely hoping that just maybe at least one finger might regain its feeling before we got home.

After riding in silence for some time The Most Interesting Man in the World looked at me and said, "I can't believe you told us to toss that fish back."

"Hey, wait a minute. That wasn't my idea" I argued.

He replied, "I don't always fish for bass, but when I do, I prefer to do it in the freezing cold and pouring rain and with a rod in my right hand and a Dos Equis beer in my left."

Interesting....

CHAPTER 20

If It Ain't Broke, Don't Fix It

Speaking of fixing something that's not broken, there is a new war that's about to break out. No, I'm not talking about the Ukraine, although those folks are coming close to melting down over there. And no, I'm not talking about a handful of crazed Republican Congressmen hell-bent on shutting down the government because they aren't getting their way.

Nope, this is much worse than either of those two conflicts. I'm talking about the Great Maple Syrup Skirmish of 2014. There are some things in this great big wonderful world that you can fuck with. You can go poking a skunk to see if you can get it to spray (it will and you will go blind). You can fuck around with your buddy and disconnect one of the six sparkplug cables so his car runs like shit until he figures it out (it's nearly impossible to even find a sparkplug cable in today's highly efficient automobiles that get nearly the same gas mileage as cars of 40 years ago).

There is one thing, however, that you don't fuck around with and that's Maple Syrup. Now I know that this book is about how to survive the economic Recovery caused by an economic Recession caused by greed and stupidity. I mean, jeezum there numbnuts, I am the one writing the damn book. And you may be scratching your head wondering what the hell Maple Syrup has to do with anything other than pancakes and French toast to say anything about recovering from a recession??

It's this inability to see past the nose on your face that has landed you in the toilet. First and foremost, Vermont Maple Syrup is everything and everything is Vermont Maple Syrup. Once you have accepted this fact as a fact, then the rest will come easy.

So what's the problem? Some brain trust has decided that the public is too stupid to comprehend the concept that Grade "B" is as good, if not better than Grade "A". It all falls back to the public school system. Forever we've been taught that if you got an "A" in math that this was better than getting a "B" in math.

Most Vermont males were thrilled if they just got through any math class without having the teacher throw a very dusty chalk eraser at their head.

When it comes to the classification of Maple Syrup, the categories are in the eyes (uh, or mouth) of the beholder. Some people like Fancy grade syrup, others like "A" light amber. Others like dark amber and still others like "B". Here's a news flash for the buying public: If it's real Vermont Maple Syrup, it's going to be delicious!

There, was that so hard? OK, so we have a bunch of different categories for our syrup. Big deal. Most Vermonters prefer "B" grade syrup simply because it's a little heartier. It's real dark and thick and sweeter than anything else on the planet. Some say it's the best syrup which is why we give it a "B" for a grade. If we gave our best syrup an "A" or worse called it Fancy, then everyone would buy it and there wouldn't be any left for us. DUH.

This has been the way things have been forever. Now comes along the National Maple Syrup Industry with this declaration: "Vermont's system for the labeling of its Maple Syrup is confusing to the public."

Really? Excuse me, but is there anyone out there who thinks that Vermonters, whose ancestors learned how to make Maple Syrup from the Indians (also known as the very first Vermonters), give a flying fuck if the public is confused? That's their problem. We all know that "B" is better than "A" because if you ever did make the mistake of getting an "A" in anything in school, your buddies would beat the shit out of you (unless of course you somehow cheated, in which case you would be idolized; but no self-respecting Vermont kid would go to such extremes for an "A". The risks were just too great.)

Below is a news article that appeared in the Huffington Post about this new classification system. To assist you in the interpretation of this story, I have included comments and observations in BOLD *Italics* (note how is just changed font so those of you who are considered to be "The Public" and presumably very easily confused, will figure out what the fuck I'm saying).

Standard Maple Syrup Grading Proposal Not So Sweet, Say Some Vermonters

By LISA RATHKE 10/07/12 11:41 AM ET **AP**

MONTPELIER, Vt. -- In a state that has a long history of maple syrup production and fiercely protects the purity of its brand, Vermont producers are proud of their "fancy," "grade A dark amber" and "grade B" syrup. *As they damn well should be!*

But the terminology has the potential to perplex consumers, particularly as Vermont's syrup production, which has boomed in the past decade, reaches broader markets. *By "broader markets" we assume they mean anything outside of the State of Vermont. Vermonters are not "perplexed" by a labeling system that goes back to the Stone Age. We thoroughly understand that a "B" is better than an "A" any day.*

So Vermont is considering joining with other syrup-producing states and Canadian provinces in selling a product with one grading standard, triggering fears by some producers that the State's vaunted brand will lose its reputation if it doesn't stand out from the rest – as they say it should. *Well, no shit Sherlock. The Vermont Brand is just about all we have left. Someone thinks fucking up our brand so that we can go lock-step with other states AND Canada is a good idea? Are you fucking kidding me? I mean, OK, Canada does have publicly financed*

[236]

healthcare and some hellacious hockey players, but they can't touch our Maple Syrup. Oh, this is such a bad idea....

"You're lumping Vermont syrup in with all the rest of them," said Kevin Bushee, 69, of the Bushee Family Maple Farm in Danby. *You tell 'em Kevin. We don't do "lumping"!*
Vermont's syrup, which forms a state industry that nets about $130 million a year, is in fact, not the same as others. The State requires that its syrup be slighter denser than other syrups because it thinks it tastes better. That requires that more sap be produced. *Bingo! You hear that? Vermont requires us to be "denser", which is why a "B" is better than an "A". Your problem could just be that you are too dense to understand this!*

Some states already use current USDA standards to grade their syrup, while others, including Vermont, have their own standards. But maple states and provinces are considering getting on board with one system, for consistency's sake. *Of course Vermont has its own standards and equally of course they are not consistent with the industry's standards. Vermont has never been consistent with anything which, by the way, it should come as no surprise, is how we have survived as a people for 250 years! Conforming to industry standards?? Are you fucking kidding me? That is just so NOT the Vermont way...*

"Most of the states are watching Vermont to see what we do," said Henry Marckres, a maple specialist with the Vermont Agency of Agriculture. *Other states (and we might as well toss in a few countries for good measure) have been watching what Vermont does on a variety of issues for hundreds of years. We're trend setters up here. OK, so Bell Bottoms started on the West Coast. There's only so much you can expect of us.*

The new standards would not affect the density which in Vermont would stay the same. And producers can do their own marketing on labels, such as calling it fancy, in addition to the

[237]

tiny grading labels. *OK, so let's see if we get this straight. The new standards won't affect density. Fine. Producers can do their own marketing on their own labels. Fine. We can still call our Fancy syrup "Fancy". Fine. We just have to add some tiny label that says our Fancy Syrup is something else. What the fuck? It's Fancy Syrup. That's what it is. If you're finding this confusing, I'm praying to God that you don't have a driver's license and actually operate a motor vehicle. Jesus-jumping-H--Christ. You're kidding, right? A new tiny label. Great.*

The four international classifications would be golden color, delicate taste; amber color, rich taste; dark color, robust taste; and very dark color, strong taste, all grade A. *Oh sure, this makes eminent sense. Take all of our Maple Syrup, light, dark, delicate, very dark, real fucking strong, goddamn near coal fucking black and call it all "A". Shit, if we used this new classification in our public schools, dipshit Johnny sitting in the back of the class who could barely tie his fucking shoes would've gotten an "A" in math.*

The change will help, not hurt, Vermont syrup sales, supporters say. *Of course it will help sales. Everything we make from damn near clear syrup to syrup that looks like motor oil will now be "A". The confused-to-the-degree-that-they-can't-put-on-their-own-underware General Public will now be able to go to the shelf where syrup is sold, drool pouring out of one side of their collective mouths like a teething one year old and say "Er….ah….duh….this must be good, because it's "A". Sweet Mother of Jesus…are we really this fucking stupid?*

"If a jug is on a shelf and if you put maple syrup from different states on the shelf, the most obvious thing is the name of the state it comes from," said Jacques Couture, a Vermont sugar maker near the Canadian border and director of the board of the Vermont Maple Sugar Makers Association. "So I don't worry at all about that detracting from Vermont's brand. Vermont's brand is what it is, and I don't think that anybody's going to take away

[238]

from that." *Well, obviously we can tell by his name that "Jacques" is a Canadian infiltrator who has somehow subverted Vermont's Maple Syrup industry. He does, however, make a valid point that people are more apt to buy VERMONT Maple Syrup, because it's from Vermont. That is true, but still…..*

The flavor descriptions are a big plus for consumers who might get confused by Vermont terms like "fancy" or "grade B," which imply that one is better than or inferior to others but really refer to strength, color or other characteristics, experts say. The ultimate choice varies from consumer to consumer, experts say. *"Experts say"?? Experts?? Who the hell is more of an expert on Vermont Maple Syrup than Vermonters who've been making VERMONT MAPLE SYRUP for 250 fucking years? Our descriptions are confusing? Consumers might be confused by Vermont's terminology?? Has there been a marketing study done to determine just how fucking dumb the consumer really is or are we just making some sort of grand assumption that the consumer could not, under any circumstances, walk and chew fucking gum at the same time? So let's get this straight. Vermont has three classifications and now we're going to five descriptions and somehow we think this dumb bastard we're calling the "Consumer" is going to be able to get their head around five descriptions? Jesus, it would be nothing short of a miracle if this dumb bastard could even find Vermont.*

"When we talk to new customers in our case on a daily basis, we almost always have to explain the difference between the grades and why the grades are called such as they are," Couture said.
People in Vermont take their syrup seriously. The State has even gotten complaints from people who bought "fancy" syrup but then complained about its delicate flavor. *Hold on just a minute. I have to go get a towel and clean up here a little bit. I think my fucking head just exploded. First of all, explaining Vermont's grading system should be seen as a plus. If it provides you with an opportunity to have a little conversation*

with this knuckle dragger who somehow was able to operate a motor vehicle and find his way to Vermont. That's a plus. Anyone dumb enough to call the State of Vermont to complain that the Fancy Syrup that they bought had too delicate a flavor should be, and I would not take this punishment lightly, beaten with rubber hoses. Someone actually called to complain about Maple Syrup? You are fucking kidding me. He shouldn't be allowed to have real Vermont Maple Syrup. He should be force-fed gallons of Aunt Jemima's fake syrup until his feet swell up like fucking balloons.

"It was just a beautiful fancy light flavor and they were used to something strong and they thought it was a fake," Marckres said. *Really? If this dumb bastard can be fooled this easily, is it any wonder we goddamn near tanked the global economy and are now suffering through what some think just might be a Recovery? Good lord.*

One apparent advantage of the new international standards for Vermont producers is the fourth grade – very dark color, strong taste – would include some of the syrup that now is sold only in bulk for processing because of the strong flavor. *News flash: if you hold a bottle of syrup up to the light and you can't see through it, it's dark, strong "B" syrup. Was that so fucking hard?*

But that bothers Bushee, too. *Goddamn right it does!*

"I don't want to see our markets get downgraded by using the commercial syrup," he said. But Jacques and others say the strong maple flavor is growing in popularity among chefs.
The change is not expected to cost producers, who have to buy labels anyway. They cost about $6 for a roll of a thousand. *Of course we don't want to downgrade the best syrup in the fucking world. Canadian infiltrator/conspirator/terrorist/communist Jacques says that chefs like stronger syrup. Well, no shit! We've been cooking with dark syrup for, oh, I don't know, 250 years or so. This is*

[240]

not news, Mr. Chef. By the way, if you get real dark, strong Maple Syrup it's fucking "B" syrup. Write that down on the back of your hand so you won't get too goddamned confused. "B" as in "Bonehead", which is how we would classify you if you can't figure out our simple classification system that's been used for generations.

The USDA plans to adopt the new terms in 2013. Neighboring New York is working with the industry to propose new regulations to incorporate the international standards, said Joe Morrissey, a New York Department of Agriculture spokesman. *Of course they are. You may recall that not too long ago, a couple of hundred years or so that it was New York that tried to take over Vermont. We were just on the threshold of forgiveness for that dastardly deed, but now this comes along. Oh, Ethan Allen….where are you now, buddy??*

Vermont will hold a series of public hearings this month. Depending on the feedback, the State agriculture secretary will decide whether or not to go ahead with rule changes to adopt the standards. *Too bad you missed this hearing. This was more fun than trying to decide whether or not we should have a doe season. If you are unfamiliar with what a doe season is, then it's no fucking wonder why you would find our classification system for Vermont Maple Syrup confusing. You're the reason they had to eliminate the stick shift and go to automatic, is my guess.*

CHAPTER 21

That's About It

OK, I've calmed down from that rant in the previous chapter. Whew, that did feel good, though.

We've come a long ways together and perhaps it's time to take stock and assess where we are. We were bumbling along nice as pie for quite some time having a ball and spending money like it was nobody's business. Life was like one big Great Gatsby party. Non-stop fun was the name of the game. Keep that champagne flowing because the clock has yet to strike midnight. It was full steam ahead and we were all having a blast.

Time is a funny thing. One day you're hangin' out with your best friend not doing much of anything other than watching him hang from an old apple tree by his nose and the next thing you know, you've got grandchildren. When the hell did THAT happen? Where'd the time go? Wait a minute, doing the math reveals that I have more sunrises behind me than I do in front of me. Whoa baby, this ain't good. I'm running out of time.

Well, it's best you relax because if it's any consolation (and it's probably not), you've been running out of time since the day you were born. It's just that it didn't seem all that relevant until you turned what 30? Maybe 40? Try 60.

So, here's the deal. The one and only thing you really would like to recover from is time and it's the only thing that you can't recover from. There you go. That's the rawest of raw deals. But then again, maybe it's not.

If you can accept the fact that you've been dying since the day you were born, the rest of living is pretty much of a cake walk. (For those of you unfamiliar with the genesis of the phrase "cake walk" it had to do with walkin' for de cake. At the age of 16, I went to the Winter Carnival at UVM and saw the various fraternities perform this feat. Young, white guys dressed up in crazy tuxedos and put on black face and high stepped across the gym floor. Yes, there really was a time when we did such things. Those days are over.)

Things come and things go. You no sooner put that long-stemmed flute on the waiter's sterling silver tray when someone taps you on the shoulder, whispers in your ear and says, "Pssst... The economy is collapsing and it appears as though you're collapsing with it."

The days of wine and roses are behind you. The world, your world, is upside down. The more air in the balloon, the louder the bang and they could hear you pop all the way over to the next county.

This is bad. In one fell swoop, life went from being pretty darned sweet to sucking. POOF, just like that. From riches to rags. From bad to worse. From the pan into the fire.

Your new reality sets in and you think to yourself, "Well, I'm screwed. There's no way out of this. I'm done. Over. Finito."

Are you really though? Isn't the way the deal works is that there's really only one gig you don't recover from and that's death. It's pretty much a given that your last day is just that, your last day. There ain't no comin' back from that one. No turn around. No comeback kid. As they say, "When you're dead, you're gone." Well, no shit.

However, in between being born and dying, if you're lucky, there's quite a span of time in which you can do all kinds of things. You can rise up. You can fall back down. You can rise up again. You can fall back down again. You can stay at the top (ugh, what an awful thought) or you can stay down on the bottom (there are many more likeminded people down here from which to choose real friends.)

You had to choose how you are going to Survive a Recession just like you have to choose how you're going to Survive a Recovery. It's always yours to have or to lose. The ball is always in your court and all you have to do is to decide whether you're going to go in for the easy layup or take the risk for that long 3-pointer. It may not seem like it at the moment of time you're in, but it's true that you make your own past and to some degree have a shot at shaping your own future.

Sure, there are plenty of things that get in the way. You may not have been the one to set the place on fire, but you sure as hell are the only one who can figure out how to get out of the burning building.

It's what we humans do. Sometimes we find ourselves in that most awful set of circumstances. Other times, we're in high clover. Anybody can survive the good times (well, OK, maybe not everybody. There are those who get totally consumed by the good times never to be heard from again). It's surviving the tough times that separates the men from the boys; the smart from the not so smart; the strong from the weak.

No one ever said this would be easy. Living isn't for the faint of heart, but put it all in perspective. Like my dad once told me, "Son, things are never as bad as they seem and they're never as good as they seem."

For a plumber born to a family that lived on dirt sandwiches, he was a pretty smart guy. Had he not smoked a zillion cigarettes, he would have lived past the age of 56. But then, that was his choice. In between his arrival day and his departure day, he packed a lot in; some of it was even good.

There's an old saying that we're all pretty much sick of but it's true: live every day like it's your last. If you can do that, you can survive just about anything. If, for some reason, you can't survive….well, then it's your last day now, isn't it?

Chart a course. Stick with it until you can't and then chart another course. If you ever find yourself confronted with a lady screaming and freaking out over a mouse….well, now you know what to do.

The End

ACKNOWLEDGEMENTS

I want to thank some folks who have made this book possible. First and foremost I want to thank the people along the way who have provided me with some great fun, long lasting memories, and of course, great stories. I've been very lucky to know some of the most amusing and interesting characters on the planet. This book represents that small space you create when you blow as hard as you can on your frost-covered windshield so you can see out just a little bit.

I want to thank Tara Dowden for using her editing skills on this book. I write like I talk, which may not necessarily make for good writing, but it sure does make for hard editing. My wife, Alison, edits my bi-monthly columns so she knows the arduous task that Tara undertook. Alison also helped to edit this book so if there's anything wrong with it you can blame these two!

For an unknown person like me to publish a book would have been impossible just a few years ago. I know this will come as a surprise, but Random House is not all that interested in my sage advice and words of rural wisdom. For that matter neither is Simon & Schuster.

Thanks to the Northshire Bookstore authors like me can get their books published. Yes, you have to do your own distribution and bust your ass to get it out to people, but it is possible. No one ever said this shit was easy.

I want to thank Alison and my kids, Meredith, Wesley and Marlan (OK, so Marlan might flunk a DNA test but he's still my kid) for no other reason than tolerating me. That's reason enough.

At the risk of having this turn into a bad Academy Award's speech (Yup, they were on last night and yup, Jennifer Lawrence fell down again. God, what a horrible thing to be remembered for; falling twice at the Oscars. That's almost as bad as our former president, George H.W. Bush puking on the Japanese leader. Jennifer's tough. She'll recover) I want to thank you, the reader.

The only thing harder than making music no one will ever hear is writing a book no one will ever read. I offer my sincere gratitude to those of you who seem to like what I do. For those of you who don't, I would offer the advice my late mom would give regarding her performances; "If you don't like it be polite and clap anyways."

If you've made it to here you've done good. Many thanks for sharing the ride.

THE AUTHOR

Bob Stannard is an eight generational Vermonter. He has served in the Vermont Legislature. He's worked as a logger, mowed lawns for a living, sold commercial real estate and worked as a lobbyist at the Vermont State House on many important issues. Mercifully, he is now retired.

He is an accomplished harmonica player and Blues singer/song writer. His musical talent has led him to perform with some of the nation's greatest Bluesmen including BB King, David Maxwell, John Hammond, Mark Hummel, Louisiana Red, David "Honey Boy" Edwards, Charlie Musselwhite and many others. Running into Jerry Portnoy in a bar in Hyannis didn't hurt either.

He has released three CDs. His most recent: "Getting Older Every Day" features the legendary Blues piano player, David Maxwell and can be purchased from his website: www.bobstannard.com You can also get this book there, too! However, since you're standing here with this book in your hand you can save yourself the cost of postage by just walking over to the counter over there and paying the nice person.

Bob is also a bi-monthly columnist for the Bennington Banner and VT Digger.

He lives in Manchester with his wife, Alison. They have two grown kids and now have four grandkids.

Aside from writing and playing music he likes to fish. He's really a pretty boring guy and wondering why on earth you'd even consider reading his books.

Contact: bob@bobstannard.com